ROCK, BACH & SUPERSCHLOCK

ROCK, BACH & SUPERSCHLOCK

HAROLD MYRA and DEAN MERRILL

A. J. HOLMAN COMPANY
division of J. B. Lippincott Company
Philadelphia and New York

Cover: Jared Lee

Book design: Ken Wolgemuth

Photographic Credits: Acme—p. 59; AP—p. 15 right; ANI—pp; 13 left, 25, 36, 37, 109; Richard L. Ball—p. 110; Bob Combs—pp. 10, 28 left, 46, 49, 61, 67, 100, 102, 103 upper, 114, 116; Rohn Engh—pp. 32, 69 upper, 87; Dave Foster—p. 113; Douglas Gilbert—pp. 34, 35, 62, 108; Steve Hoke—pp. 101 upper, 103 lower; Richard T. Lee—pp. 101 lower, 105; Lutheran Film Associates—p. 91; United Methodist Information—p. 94; University of Wisconsin—p. 50; UPI—pp. 14, 15 left, 16, 22, 23, 26, 47; Ed Wallowitch—pp. 48, 64, 65 lower, 68, 84, 85.

Song lyric credits: "Taxman" and "Love You To" pp. 56, 57, copyright © 1966 Northern Songs, Ltd. Used by Permission. All rights reserved. "Too Darn Hot" pp· 58, 59, copyright © 1949 by Cole Porter. Reprinted by permission of the publisher, T. B. Harms Company. "I Wish We'd All Been Ready" p. 112, copyright © 1969 Beechwood Music Corporation / J. C. Love Publishing Company. Used by permission. "Little Country Church" p. 114, copyright © 1971 Dunamis Music. All rights administered by United Artists Music Co. Inc., New York, N. Y. 10019. Used by permission.

U. S. Library of Congress Cataloging in Publication Data

Myra, Harold Lawrence, birth date
Rock, Bach & Superschlock.

1. Religion and music. I. Merrill, Dean, joint author. II. Title.
ML3865.M97   780'.09   71-39852
ISBN-0-87981-007-6

CHAPTERS

ABOUT THE AUTHORS

Harold Myra, 32, is a twelve-year veteran journalist, editor of *Campus Life* Magazine and Youth for Christ Vice-President for Literature since 1965. Not technically musical, he has nevertheless written the lyrics for several songs as well as *The Carpenter*, a 1972 musical drama about the God-Man from Nazareth. Listed in *Who's Who in the Midwest*, he is also the author of *No Man in Eden*, a space novel, and *Michelle, You Scalawag, I Love You*, a poetic frolic about his daughter's first year.

Dean Merrill, 28, came to *Campus Life* about the time Myra took over, left four years later to get his M.A. in journalism at Syracuse University, and is now back as a senior editor. He was chosen to sing, play guitar and piano on a YFC Teen Team tour to Europe and Israel in 1964. Presently, he leads congregational singing in his church on Sundays, and occasionally plays organ. He and his wife sing together and provide their own accompaniment; they're also the parents of a teen-age niece.

ROCK, BACH & SUPERSCHLOCK

Chuck Berry

10

THE ROCK REVOLUTION

Rock music. That's a good word for it. *Rock.* It not only describes the sound . . . and what kids do when they hear it . . . but the total effect it's had on civilized man. Ever since 1954, when a slightly over-the-hill country and western group named Bill Haley and the Comets stumbled onto "Rock around the Clock" — the entire music industry and its customers have been doing just that.

It's been quite a jolt.

It was supposed to be a passing fad . . . Elvis, Chuck Berry, Buddy Holly and Jerry Lee Lewis, the Everly Brothers. But the fad wouldn't fade.

It added some quieter variations during the folk music revival of 1959-63 . . . the Kingston Trio, the New Christy Minstrels, Woody Guthrie's songs being sung by Joan Baez, Peter, Paul and Mary, and young Bob Dylan.

It assaulted the common standards of propriety: CBS cameramen were ordered not to show Elvis below the waist. Dick Clark found himself answering to the United States Congress for the Payola scandals. Chiropractors found themselves repairing the tortured sacroiliacs of the nation's Twisters.

But all that was only a prelude for the songs to come. . . .

1964

"I want to hold your hand"

They were here the first time for only two weeks, but Ed Sullivan nabbed them for both Sunday nights. (He'd learned his lesson a few years earlier with Elvis, whom he had at first condemned as "unfit for a family audience," but two months later paid $50,000 for three brief appearances.)

John F. Kennedy had been in his grave not yet three months. A pall of grief and self-doubt hung over the country. It was still winter.

The four Liverpudlians who arrived at Kennedy International Airport on Friday, February 7, 1964, were just the opposite. Coming off two years of conquest in Britain, they were now ready to spread their raucous hilarity to the colonies: "I want to hold your hand . . . yeah, yeah, yeah."

The song jumped from number forty-five on *Billboard's* national hit parade to number one — and stayed there for seven straight weeks. Over one million orders were received in the first ten days. Everywhere the Beatles traveled, girls shrieked, mothers fumed about the shaggy hair, policemen plugged their ears, and Capitol Records raked in the coins. An estimated sixty percent of all singles sold during the first three months were by the Beatles.

When they appeared on "The Ed Sullivan Show," an astonishing seventy-three million people watched — nearly half the population. The next day the *Washington Post* commented, "Don't knock the Beatles; during the hour when they were on Ed Sullivan's show, there wasn't a hub-

cap stolen anywhere in America." There was plenty of damage at the live concerts, however, when teen-age throngs went berserk.

"I Want to Hold Your Hand" was not a fluke. More smash hits kept coming; nobody before or since has turned out so many winners in a row. By the first of April, the Beatles had captured the top five slots all at once:

1. "Can't Buy Me Love"
2. "Twist and Shout"
3. "She Loves You"
4. "I Want to Hold Your Hand"
5. "Please Please Me"

Never before had Americans gone so wild over foreigners in the field

"the sound of silence"

well as its attitude was best represented by Simon and Garfunkel, who sang about barriers ("people hearing without listening") and the despair of not finding a communication bridge.

The obscure profundity of Paul Simon was, at least in part, the consequence of Bob Dylan, whose songs were touching almost every nerve ending in American life: prejudice, war, the Bomb, shallowness, the law, the federal government, drugs. Lyrics were becoming so important they were actually being printed on the record jackets. It was a time for saying things.

1967
Sgt. Pepper's
lonely hearts club band

The crescendo that had been building for nearly four years reached its peak with the Beatle's thirteenth album, *Sgt. Pepper*, and others like it: Dylan's *Blonde on Blonde*, the Rolling Stones' *Their Satanic Majesties Request*, Jefferson Airplane's *Surrealistic Pillow*.

The center of action had shifted to the album, leaving the hit-single bag largely to plastic groups like the Monkees (chosen the year before by promoters who placed newspaper ads to find four warm bodies to imitate *A Hard Day's Night* in a television serial). Indeed, the biggest selling single of the year was a bubblegum ditty called "The Letter" by the Boxtops.

Meanwhile, out of teenybopper range, *Sgt. Pepper* touched the really heavy bases of companionship, family hassles, world-changing, boredom, tripping out ("I'd love to turn you on").

That line promptly got the song banned by the BBC. Many adults began to take the Beatles seriously once they heard *Sgt. Pepper*. It was more than an album; with one song sometimes running right into another, it was almost a rock symphony. Leonard Bernstein, conductor of the New York Philharmonic, thought it was "possibly one of the greatest musical works of all time."

Actually, some listeners saw more in it than did the Beatles themselves; John Lennon in a later interview remarked that the last song, "A Day in the Life" was actually two tunes stuck together, one of Paul's and one of his own written while reading a newspaper. "We have a film of

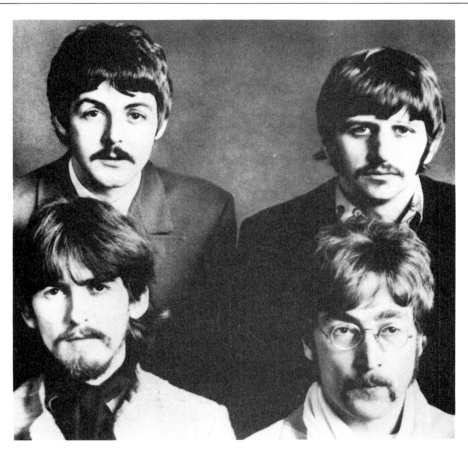

No more tours, no more pandemonium, not even many smiles . . . the Beatles had entered phase two.

doing it in the studio," he said, "Everybody was there — the Stones and the whole swinging London, all dressed in masks and stoned out of their skulls. . . . We got everybody crackers and did it. It was great. The final chord, the final freak out, like the end of the world — that was about ten of us pounding. . . ."

1968   "Mrs. Robinson"

What next? Total incoherence? Silence? No, a return to the old days. *Sgt. Pepper* was followed by a double album simply called *The Beatles,* a tribute to the history of rock. Bob Dylan went back to his acoustic guitar and harmonica for *John Wesley Harding* and then *Nashville Skyline.* The Stones relaxed with *Beggars' Banquet.* Some groups — Cream, Big Brother and the Holding Company, the Who, the Doors — kept screaming for another year, but the progressive era was winding down.

The caskets coming home from Vietnam were joined by a casket for Martin Luther King, and two months later, one for Robert F. Kennedy. It was a violent year, students making a final lunge for the political levers at the Democratic National Convention in Chicago — and failing. The analogy of a mental institution in "Mrs. Robinson," again by Simon and Garfunkel, was poignant. The last refrain ("Where have you gone, Joe DiMaggio? . . .) was not really about a retired baseball player, but about the lack of heroes.

They were veteran balladeers now, a long way from 1957 when they came out of Queens with flattop haircuts and a one-shot hit, "Hey Schoolgirl."

S & G had three top-selling albums that year: "The Graduate" Soundtrack (number two), Bookends (number four) and Parsley, Sage, Rosemary and Thyme (number six). College students especially found them articulate as the Nixon era began.

plus...Hair

"The American tribal love rock musical," it was billed, the music being a backdrop for the most skin and filth Broadway had ever seen. "Aquarius," "Let the Sunshine In," "Hair" and "Good Morning Starshine" all hit the Top Ten. Since its opening on April 29, 1968, Hair has been staged all over the country and overseas as well; it's still grossing over $18 million a year.

The flag becomes
a handy
hammock in one
of Hair's milder insults.

1969

Woodstock Festival

"Three days of peace and music" was the selling slogan — and it sold. By the droves and masses they came, nearly half a million in all, temporarily creating the third largest city in the state of New York right there on Max Yasgur's hillside.

They heard twenty-nine top acts — everyone from happy John Sebastian, to sweaty Joe Cocker, to histrionic Ten Years After, to pregnant Joan Baez, to easygoing Arlo Guthrie, to dramatic Jimi Hendrix who made an instrumental solo out of the national anthem.

Very few of them paid the eighteen dollar admission fee that was supposed to float the event (as a result, the promoters lost a cool 1.4 million dollars). Nearly everyone got wet, and hungry, and filthy in the mud, and tired of grubbing for the necessities of life. A fair number of them got high from the assortment of marijuana, pills and other drugs that was readily available. Dozens had bad trips. One young woman had a baby.

The crowd wasn't really interested in revolution; when Abbie Hoffman, one of the Chicago Seven, grabbed a mike to raise support for John Sinclair in jail, Peter Townshend of the Who promptly hit him with his guitar. After all, the point was entertainment — and to the entertainers, the point was money. Though the crowd didn't know it, the frequent delays between acts were caused by demands of "Cash NOW!" backstage before the groups came on to proclaim love and brotherhood.

It was a never-to-be-repeated happening that generated a fantastic togetherness among the listeners (if not the singers). Some tried to recreate the magic in December at Altamont Speedway near San Francisco. Three hundred thousand showed up for the one-day "free festival" to hear the Rolling Stones; before it was over a young man had been murdered within yards of the stage.

1970

Jesus Christ Superstar

The Jesus-trend got a gradual start; "Let It Be," by the Beatles (sampling yet another religion) was a hymn to the Virgin Mary and was soon followed by Norman Greenbaum's "Spirit in the Sky." The chorus lyric, "Gotta have a friend in Jesus," was not Greenbaum's conviction; he sim-

On Broadway, the masses appeal to the Superstar.

ply wanted to try his hand at writing a religious hit. He succeeded.

Two young Englishmen, Andrew Lloyd Webber and Tim Rice, came at it much the same way, casually trying to figure out just what Christ was all about. But their hit turned out to be eighty-seven minutes long — a full rock opera called *Jesus Christ Superstar* that painted Jesus as a harried fanatic being done in by a worried Judas. It was a very dramatic version of Christ's last seven days — minus His divinity and His resurrection. Even so, it carried fantastic wallop, even reverence, especially at the end. It sold more than 2.5 million copies at $9.98 a crack.

Christians, of course, promptly announced that this was not the Christ of the New Testament, but a distortion. That didn't bother Webber and Rice much; they had intended their work to be a question, not an answer. When on "The David Frost Show" a year later they were asked what was the most significant line in *Superstar,* they quickly pointed to Judas' final plea: "Don't you get me wrong — I only want to know."

Tim Rice, who wrote those words, explained it all when he said, "It happens that we don't see Christ as God but as simply the right man at the right time in the right place." Why didn't they include the Resurrection? "Well, that's getting over into subjectivity and myth, we felt."

The work was later turned into an outlandish off-Broadway production, with Christ (Jeff Fenholt, 21) rising from the stage floor in a glittering 20,000 dollar robe, and dying not on a cross but a huge tilted golden triangle that slowly projected toward the audience. "By the end of the evening," Fenholt said once, "I'm almost hating the crowd. They're out there applauding, but they're exactly the types who would have crucified Christ."

1971

Paul Stookey

James Taylor

28

"Fire and Rain"

God-rock was stronger than ever in 1971, with George Harrison's "My Sweet Lord" and Judy Collins' "Amazing Grace." Some churchgoers wondered, "What's that hymn doing on the rock stations?" (Their predecessors, two centuries earlier, had asked John Newton, "What's that secular tune doing with your hymn?") Jethro Tull took the entire second side of *Aqualung* to ask who God is and to vent disgust at how people have distorted Him.

Others were more positive. Marvin Gaye, an established Motown star, did an album called *What's Going On* that stated his faith in clear language — and was listed among *Time* Magazine's "Best LPs of the Year," Paul Stookey, who earlier in "Hymn" had told about trips to sterile churches ("All that I could say was, 'I believe in You' "), came out with "The Wedding Song," inviting Jesus to attend. *Godspell,* another rock musical on Broadway, was closer to the Jesus of St. Matthew's Gospel, and better done, said a number of critics.

James Taylor occasionally mentioned Jesus, but he stood tall in '71 more as the epitome of the quiet, pensive, brooding solo poet. After a year on drugs in New York City and two stints in mental hospitals, he was hardly in position to claim all the answers, but only some of the more important questions and concerns. "Fire and Rain" at first appears to be disjointed, the verses unrelated to each other. Actually, each recalls a lonely time in the young troubadour's life; together, they add up to a call for help.

1972 ▮▮▮▮

Is rock starting to crumble? Some say we've come to the end of an era, that the '70s are much different from the '60s, and that rock is all over. Others say the boulder is only changing shape as it gets squeezed by the despair and apathy of the times.

One thing is for sure: the supergroups are breaking up. Cream, the Yardbirds, Jimi Hendrix Experience, the Beatles — the list keeps getting longer. Even people like Simon and Garfunkel, and Peter, Paul and Mary have split. "The dream is over," said John Lennon in 1971. "I'm not just talking about the Beatles. I'm talking about the generation thing. It's over, and we gotta — I have personally gotta — get down to so-called reality."

Actually, it's easy to see that the first great stars such as Lennon are getting older and finding themselves on the uncomfortable side of their earlier advice, "Don't trust anyone over thirty." Some continue to sing by themselves, joining the ranks of the young balladeers like Elton John, Cat

Stevens, James Taylor and his brothers. Others drop completely out of sight.

In fact, the top song of 1972 may turn out to be the nostalgic "American Pie," by Don McLean. What each line means is anybody's guess, but the unmistakable overall feeling is that the good old days are gone. He begins, "Long, long time ago, I can still remember how that music used to make me smile . . ." and winds through brainteasing images of high-school sock hops, court jesters, halftime marching bands and satanic fire. It's all a eulogy for what happened before "the day the music died."

Yet is it really dead? Young people are now firmly in the habit of expressing themselves through music, and probably won't soon give it up. It will be a long time before we return to a situation like the 1940s, when older adults manipulated the pop music scene. The sounds may fluctuate, amplifiers may come and go, groups may jell and melt, but music will continue to be the language of the young.

Yet millions of people (of all ages) listen to music, sing it, love it, criticize it, spend money on it — without understanding how it works. Where it comes from. How its pieces are put together. How it moves them.

Which is precisely why this book was written.

CHAPTER TWO

Young music
is not
made
by strings
alone,
of course . . .

but it could never live without them.
Simple strands of steel, nylon or gut,
usually wrapped in metal alloy,
and stretched as if on a medieval torturing rack . . .
their cries are the foundation sounds upon which
rock, folk, soul, country and even some classics are built.

They can be as quiet as the acoustic guitar
of young Janis Ian,
softly tuning
in a studio corner . . .
or they can
be multiplied by
banks of
amplifiers behind
Michael Davis
of MC5 to
fill all of
Chicago's
Soldier Field.

35

36

The strings come four at a time . . . or five, or six, or eight, or twelve, or even more. David Brown of Santana appears to have his hands full with the minimum . . . what would he do with Ravi Shankar's sitar? Perhaps in no other trade must apprentices work so long at mastering the tools.

A BAG OF TRICKS

Zzzzzzz!

There's a fly in the room.

A tickling, irritating, pesky fly.

A filthy, germ-carrying fly.

A nervous, ever-cruising, hard-to-kill fly.

Your brain gets all that information from a zzzzzzz sound . . . a simple rasping tone pitched somewhere around low C, fading in and out as the fly circles.

But imagine for a moment that you're deaf. You don't hear the zzzzzzz. You don't think about a fly at all. You don't worry about germs. You don't get up and get a fly-swatter. You don't do anything, unless you happen to look up and see the fly instead.

You miss out on the entire world of sounds, and all that they mean.

But if you can hear, you know that you're at the vortex of a continual hurricane of sounds and clanks and rattles and whooshes and plinks and scrapes and shrieks and hums and thumps. Occasionally, some of these get organized enough to show some kind of pattern.

That's music.

Now the boundaries of all this are sort of fuzzy. What's music and what's just plain racket? Well, that's a matter of opinion, depending on whether you're an American or a Fiji Islander, whether you're seventeen or seventy, whether you're a student of what lots of other people have called music over the years or whether you're not.

Bach's *Fugue in D Minor*? Yes, that's definitely musical.

Three Dog Night singing "Joy to the World"? Likewise.

Martin Luther King preaching a sermon? Well, some listeners definitely heard rhythm patterns and a subtle, quavering melody line as he spoke. "Sing-song," they called it. Others heard only the words.

A fly buzzing in a room? Once again, it all depends on the listener. Two flies playing tag with each other in an otherwise quiet room? A duet!

But a composer doesn't often resort to using pairs of buzzing flies. He has so many tricks in his bag of sounds that are easier to control. To start with, he has the noises the human larynx can make — low growls, high squeaks, whispers, roars, in male or female shades. Not a bad start.

But the musician has lots of other sound-tricks at his fingertips. He can use wind-power to rush through everything from flutes to trumpets to saxophones to tubas or even pipe organs, which demand the most wind of all. (One of the early organs at Winchester Cathedral in England needed seventy men pumping hard to fill its 400 pipes! All that for only ten different notes; the keys were wide enough to be mashed down by the fist of the man called the "organ-beater.")

Even more sounds come from tightened strings on violins and guitars, basses and pianos. If the musician wants them louder, he can amplify the vibrations electronically through a combination of transistors and speaker cones. In fact, electronic gadgetry can imitate almost every sound in the bag — even percussion sounds like drums and tambourines — through an electric organ, for example.

And with this mighty array of tools, the composer goes to work. A little of this, a little of that, some of the other, a lot of this . . . the combinations, obviously, are unlimited. He is much like a painter with his canvas, oils and brushes . . . or a sculptor with his clay, wood, stone, bronze and chisels . . . or a housewife with her cloth, scissors, needles and thread. The materials are no big deal. The genius shows up in how they're put together.

Nowhere is this more evident than in the new field of electronic music. Back in 1952, two professors at Columbia University began fooling around with tape recorders. Vladimir Ussachevsky and Otto Luening recorded all kinds of sounds — not only instruments, but doors slamming, feet shuffling, anything — to see if they could make something musical out of them.

Ussachevsky spliced together what he called "A Piece for Tape Recorder" using a gong, a single stroke on a cymbal, the noise of a jet plane, a few organ chords, some piano notes, and one thump on a kettledrum which he distorted into a wind-like sound! In addition, he used four

Three Dog Night, whose "Joy to the World" was the hottest selling single in America in 1971. (Their name allegedly comes from Australia's "outback," where aborigines sleep with their dogs huddled around them for warmth. Thus, a "three dog night" is a very cold one.)

pure tones produced on an oscillator. One is a simple hum; another he calls "white noise" — it sounds like static on an old worn-out radio. A third he calls "sawtooth," because it kind of grates on you. Finally, he threw in a tremolo sound he got by tinkering with the click of a switch on (what else?) his tape recorder.

But you'd never recognize any of that by listening to the piece. The sounds have been re-recorded backwards, or at the wrong speed, or filtered to remove some of the harmonics, or reverberated beyond recognition. At times the composer even snipped off the initial attack and used only the "tail" of the sound, so that the cymbal, for example, comes out like a quiet drone.

But all together, it still *feels* like music. It has an eerie, far-out-in-space effect to it. That's because Ussachevsky kept from going insane with his little bits and pieces of tape long enough to give them some coherence, some unity. In a strange sense, he actually "recycled" noise into something useful and beautiful again.

(What *did* nearly unglue the professor was trying to get a copyright on his work. The Copyright Office demanded that he write down his piece in ordinary musical notation. Translating all his buzzes and whirrs and rasps onto musical staff lines took him forty hours!)

Since then, others have experimented with new sounds for the bag of tricks, some even employing a computer. They program how many notes they want at a time, in what rhythm, using certain intervals, and then let the computer choose at random within those guidelines. They've come up with some fascinating "music." Not as good as a human can do, say the flesh-and-blood composers, of course . . . but nevertheless interesting.

All this flirtation between music and electronics has finally brought us to a marriage in the new things called synthesizers. The first ones, the Moogs, have been joined by the more advanced Arp synthesizers, which produce amazing new sounds and are essentially an altogether new class of instrument for the bag of tricks.

So rock music shares a common source with all other styles and, in fact, is hardly the most eccentric. It is not some weird, unnatural, malignant format threatening to gobble up all the pure, lovely, God-intended kinds. Paul McCartney, Bob Dylan and Sly Stone have used the same instruments as everyone else — only in a way that has captured young imaginations the past few years.

Actually, anyone can do it. You use amplified guitars, amplified basses, heavy percussion (drums, cymbals, tambourines, etc.), add a little mouth organ or even electronic organ if you want — and you've got what we call a *rock* sound.

The other styles are not much different. Hold back the percussion a little bit, keep the guitar chords simple and make them go *twang!* on the ends, replace the organ with fancy-fingered violins (only call them "fiddles" instead) — and you have produced what is known as a *country and western* sound.

Throw out the amplifiers and use only acoustical guitars, or at least very subdued electric ones — and it sounds like *folk*.

Use brass instruments — trumpets, saxophones — instead of strings as your foundation, back them up with a certain type of piano technique, restore the percussion fairly strong, and turn everybody loose to improvise on a given melody — you've created *jazz*.

Use the full range of instruments, but nail the players down to only written notes on the page — no messing around out of their own heads — and if you really know what you're doing, you can create a *symphonic* sound.

The list could go on and on — soul, pop, easy listening, mood — and if you start digging back into history or across into other cultures, you find more and more musical formats that are unfamiliar to us today.

What do the sounds from the musician's bag of tricks do to you?

Some people say, "Nothing. I'm not affected by music. I couldn't tell you the name of a single tune. I can take it or leave it."

Nonsense. Everyone is affected by music. Even without words. And rock audiences weren't the first to be overcome by music. More than a century ago, Franz Liszt, the noted Hungarian composer-pianist, was known for branching off from the written scores of other people's music so he could show off his fiery technique. Mature women screamed and fainted at his concerts, it was so exciting. The first time the concert-goers of Paris heard Igor Stravinsky's new *Le Sacre du Printemps* around 1913, they rioted over his earth-cleaving chords.

The impressions we get from sounds alone are powerful. Every time you walk into a supermarket, you're surrounded by music. It's part of the fixtures, as much as the fluorescent lighting or anything else.

And it's not just any type of music, either. No lush, dreamy, take-your-time orchestras. It's happy music. Go-go-go. Buy-buy-buy. Spend your money, folks, have a good time, and isn't it fun to be throwing all these things into the cart?!

But when you go to your dentist, it's a different story. The music turns quieter, more soothing, something to take your mind off the awaiting disasters. Scientific studies have proven that dental patients feel (or at least demonstrate) less pain when easy-listening-type music is piped into the office.

Even the airlines try to turn each landing and takeoff into a good-time hour by using recorded music. If you've never flown before, you may be sitting there in the terminal scared to death . . . but when you walk onto the plane, the music tells you to relax and it's so nice to have you in the Friendly Skies. At the end of the flight, the stewardesses, in between picking up everyone's plastic cups and bugging them to fasten seat belts, must remember to switch on the music once again, so that you feel as if you're walking out of a theater or a wedding.

You only have to go to a funeral once to know that music *does something* to people. The mourners are, of course, right on the brink of an emotional expression — in this case, grief — and often what gives them the final nudge is music. A singer may use almost the exact words as the minister who speaks — yet people begin to weep when those words are combined with music. For that reason, some people insist that music should be left out of funerals. That, of course, is based on their assumption that everybody should try to keep the lid on their emotions about death.

Musical response is probably most obvious in little children. They react to the *impressions* of music long before they can understand the words. Have you ever watched a two-year-old stand in the middle of a liv-

Bob Dylan . . .
the man the folk fans
booed off the stage
at the 1965
Newport Folk Festival
because he had dared
to walk on with
an amplified guitar.

ing room floor and dance his own private jig to the rhythm of the radio or stereo? Where did he learn that? Certainly not from his dignified parents! The little toddler simply *feels* it on the inside. The rhythm creates an anticipation . . . he knows when the next thump is going to occur, and his whole body is tense until it comes. In fact, he may go on bouncing an extra beat or two after the song ends, simply because he was expecting it so much!

Other infants begin to cry whenever they hear music in a minor key. Why? They simply get a sensation of sadness from it.

Before a child is a year old, he's already starting to build music memories. He remembers the last time his mommy sang him to sleep, and it felt good, and he wants to enjoy that feeling again. In the years to come, he'll be collecting huge numbers of such memories.

So the people who claim to be unaffected by music are usually people who have suppressed their power to imagine. Because imagining is what musical sound is all about. That's what they teach you to do in music appreciation classes; they say, "Don't just sit there and think, 'Stupid highbrow music!' over and over. During this final waltz of *The Nutcracker* by Tchaikovsky, visualize a beehive working overtime on the honey shift. Let the music paint a mental picture for you."

The imaginations we come up with via music can run the full gamut of our moods. Joy, happiness, frivolity, daydreaming, fear, frustration, anger, pride, tension, pathos, frenzy — they come through, whether it's a symphony or acid rock.

It's a deep-down kind of thing that will probably never be fully explained. Over twenty years ago, the Indiana State Hospital at Indianapolis shelled out 5,000 dollars for a piped-in music system. Each night at bedtime they played soothing music to the mental patients there. Within two years the savings on torn bedding alone paid for the entire system! In many other mental hospitals, the attendants have noticed that fighting, pushing and quarreling stops — and even table manners improve — when soft music, particularly light semi-classics, are played at mealtime.

Popular Science once told of an epileptic woman who could cancel seizures by taking "doses" of music when she felt an attack coming. A European scientist, S. V. Kravkov, found that music could often improve eyesight by as much as twenty-five percent.

In factories, businessmen have learned that music is a great help on assembly line jobs or other boring tasks. The British first tried it during World War II in the munitions plants and raised production 6.2 percent at the least, 11.3 percent at the most. One of the girls admitted, "It makes you work better because you talk less."

You don't have to believe this next one if you don't want to, but there is firm scientific evidence that musical sounds even affect *plants!* George E. Smith, a farmer near Normal, Ill., played Gershwin's "Rhapsody in Blue" as well as some other selections twenty-four hours a day during a growing season — and raised his corn production by more than twenty bushels an acre. (The corn, however, liked a single continuous low note even better than Gershwin, and produced 29.6 more bushels per acre as compared to a "silent" plot. Which only goes to show that you never know what will appeal to corn ears.)

Dr. T. C. N. Singh, head of the department of botany at Annamalai University in India, has done extensive experiments on rice, tobacco, tapioca, sugarcane and cotton. Music boosted yields from twenty-five to sixty-five percent.

And more recently, two Canadian botanists treated wheat seedlings to continuous tones. Without exception, the plants turned out two or three times as large, with nearly four times as many shoots on them, as the ones which got no concert. If things keep going this well, the botanists say,

Little Stevie Wonder,
a Motown ambassador
of soul music.

"For only 300 dollars a small farmer could buy an oscillator and a speaker to stimulate his wheat into highly profitable growth."

What if you played rock music for the plants? Would they die of shock? Would they be charged up to grow even faster? An experimenter in Chicago several years ago had two cows fitted with headsets; one heard the local rock station, the other an easy listening station. The soft-music cow allegedly gave more milk throughout the test period!

Whether that proves anything is anyone's debate. It's probably more to the point to talk about how humans respond to rock. If you're an adult who's accustomed to quieter, more soothing styles, you quickly get a headache. But if rock is your standard diet, you decide what is "loud" and "soft," what is "happy" and what is "meditative" only within the rock frame.

It's just like other kinds of music: an "up-tempo" song in a Baptist church in New York turns out to be only "medium" in a Baptist church in Texas. It all depends on your frame of reference.

Rock, as it has developed over the last two decades, is generally

Pity the poor microphone when Janis Joplin put down her bottle of Southern Comfort and launched into one of her all-out squeals.

louder than some other styles. Why? Because it's the music of the young, and young people are louder and more vigorous about almost everything they do. The kid comes home from school and wants some excitement; he likes his music turned up. His dad comes home from work where both people and machinery have been yelling at him all day long, and he'd like "a little peace and quiet, O.K.?" You can't really blame either one for being frustrated with the other.

Some physicians have proved that heavy concert rock (as well as jet aircraft engines and jackhammers on road construction projects) can be simply *too* loud for the human eardrum to endure for very long. They measure it in units of loudness call decibels. And their conclusions have been verified by the fact that some rock musicians, who play really loud night after night, have started to have hearing problems. In at least one test, teen-agers who were steady rock concert-goers were found unable to hear birds or crickets in a meadow.

Otherwise, loudness is subject, like most other things, to the law of diminishing returns. The first time you hear a heavy band, you're awestruck by the massive sound. You can't think of anything else; you're captivated. All else is blotted out.

But the next time, the effect isn't quite so much. The next time, a little less. Before long, you're back to normal; your brain has adjusted to the point that you respond the same whether you're hearing the group live or watching them on television (with nothing but a dinky six-inch speaker to carry the music!).

Rock also tends to have more predominant rhythms than other styles, but that again is an entirely relative thing. James L. Mursell, in *The Psychology of Music,* says, "It is not true that we find any correlation between the pulse or the breath rate and the pattern of the music." In other words, the rhythm *does not* make you breathe faster or your heart beat differently unless you are also responding to the notes and the words and the whole musical experience. If you want to ignore it, it can't reach out there and hypnotize you.

Perhaps the most unfortunate thing that happens is that people invariably choose their favorite styles from the bag of tricks and begin knocking everything else. Kids defend rock; their parents like what they get on FM radio; their grandparents swear by the golden oldies of the 1920s. And very quickly, the whole scene becomes polarized. It breaks down into "my music" and "your music," "my radio station" and "your radio station" — and, of course, "my" choices are better and "yours" are really out of it.

The net result? Great sections of the bag of tricks go ignored, and lots of good listening is lost. A few summers ago, a *Campus Life* Magazine editor guided a teen tour to Europe for three weeks. On the last night in Rome, the travel agency had arranged for the group to take in an authentic Italian opera, *Aida,* at the famous outdoor amphitheater, the Baths of Caracalla.

Ahead of time, the editor told the students, "O.K., I know opera isn't exactly your favorite bag. Tonight's performance will be in Italian. not English. But you'll receive a program printed in English, and by reading the synopsis before each scene, you can still figure out what's going on. Let's stretch our minds a little to see if we can take in a different musical format."

The opera began around 9:00 P.M.. and lasted until nearly 1:00 A.M. The split in the group was unmistakable. Half of them were scrutinizing their programs, following the actors through binoculars, and shouting "Bravo!" after the arias right along with the most avid Roman opera buffs. For them it was a whole new vista in music.

The other half were bored to death. They yawned, they fell asleep, they complained about the hard seats. The operatic section of the bag of tricks was simply too much for them to appreciate.

Another form of musical bigotry.

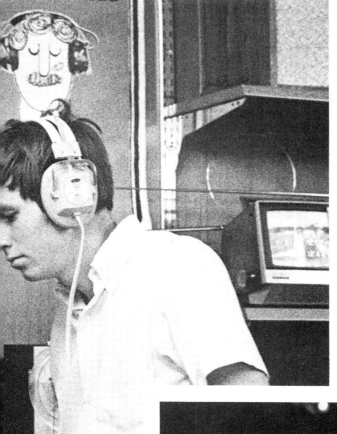

Music, music—its tide sweeps the world, with the greatest flooding in the United States. Americans, who spent half a billion dollars on records in 1960, now spend three times that much.

Choosing, selecting, sorting in the midst of the blitz —that's the toughest part of all. What is worth one's money, one's time? What is nothing but schlock?

The other arts — literature, photography,
painting, theater, sculpture, film,
even television — are mixed bags as well.

The good and the evil, the profound and
the insipid come side by side
in a never-ending parade of options.

WHATEVER HAPPENED TO "SATAN'S SEVENTH"?

"The loud sounds and bright lights of today are tremendous indoc-
trination tools. . . . If the right kind of beat makes you tap your foot,
what kind of beat makes you curl your fist and strike?"
—Frank Zappa of the Mothers of
Invention in a *Life* Magazine article.

"It ought to be apparent to every sincere Bible-believing Christian
that *(Jesus Christ Superstar)* is a gigantic blasphemy. . . . Don't let
anyone deceive you into thinking it has value, no matter who quotes
it or plays it. The rock music that accompanies it is, of course, a blasphemy itself. Be alert . . . recognize the work of Satan."
—a Kansas church newsletter.

"Eeeeeaughhhhhhhhooooooooooooooooooeeeeyyeahhhhh!!!!"
—New York City girls welcoming the
Beatles to America, February 7, 1964.

"The only Christian thing for you, young person, is total abstinence
from rock music stations and the destruction of every hard rock
record you own."
—Bob Larson, anti-rock crusader.

Wow! People *do* get excited about music. At times over the past fifteen years, the shouting match between the fans and the critics of rock has raged almost louder than the music itself. Parents and teen-agers have argued about it, professional musicians have groaned over it, and even congressional committees have held hearings on it.

It's not the first time, however, for such struggles. More than 500 years before Christ, a Greek philosopher walked by a blacksmith's shop. His name was Pythagoras (remember him from geoometry? He's the guy who first figured out how to measure the third side of a right-angle triangle.). The clanging sounds of the hammer blows intrigued him; he began thinking about tones and intervals, the distances between tones. After playing around for a while with the mathematics involved, Pythagoras and his pupils decided that octaves (two notes with the same letter-name, like "C" and "high C") not only sounded pretty good but "reflected the mathematical order in the universe" — whatever that means! To Pythagoras, it meant that an octave was a "good" interval. The same was true of fifths (like "C" and the "G" above it) and fourths ("C" and the next "F," for example).

The rest of the intervals were bad news, they said. They just didn't match up with the planets or something. So if you and your friend were singing and happened to hit a third or a sixth — shame on you.

Aristoxenus was another Greek thinker who came along around 100 years later, and he said to forget all that mathematical jive and just go by whatever sounds pleasing. The whole thing was relative to what your ear told you, anyway, he claimed. The Pythagoreans didn't think much of that idea, and the Greeks of that time, who generally enjoyed digging for profound meanings in simple things, sort of gave Aristoxenus a cold reception.

The hang-up on "good" and "bad" intervals somehow survived to Christian times — but with different rationales. The third — which, if you've ever sung "Three Blind Mice" as a round, is what you hear constantly — was off limits *because it represented the Holy Trinity!* The early chants and hymns were written largely using fourths and fifths.

The really bad no-no was the seventh — one note shy of an octave. According to the church fathers, it "excited the flesh," and therefore was banned under the name of "Satan's seventh."

All of this was about as important to the art of music as the color of toothbrushes!

Finally, after far too many centuries, we've realized that musical sounds are merely tools and cannot be good or evil in themselves. They are only what the composer happened to pull out of his bag of tricks. To talk about chords or melodies or rhythm patterns as if they had moral natures is about as far-out as a carpenter worrying over the goodness or evilness inside his hammer, chisels, saw, plane or square!

This does not mean that we cannot make some judgments about G-major chords, 3/4 tempos or octave jumps. We can, but not in any moral or eternal sense. We can judge music on how it appears to us —

Is it beautiful or irritating?

Is it varied or monotonous?

Is it loud or soft?

Is it cohesive or jumbled?

— and a lot more. We might not be able to convince very many other human beings to agree with our evaluations, but so what? We have defined the music according to our own criteria. There's nothing moral or immoral about any of the above; life itself is at times irritating, monotonous or jumbled, and it is neither right nor wrong for sounds to mirror that.

Judging technique is what keeps the music critics for newspapers and magazines busy earning a living. Their perceptions are supposed to be sharper than the rest of ours, so that we find it interesting to read what they think of new music as it comes along. Then we promptly turn around and shrug, "Well, that's one man's opinion!"

As for the sounds themselves, they get used over and over again, in all sorts of contexts, and there is no honest way to attach guilt by association. For example, around 1780 a London organist named John Stafford Smith wrote an eight-line tune to be used by the boys down at the pub as a drinking song. They called themselves the Anacreontic Society of London, after Anacreon, the Greek poet who wrote mostly about women and wine.

The society's president, Ralph Tomlinson, wrote some words to go with the tune, the last line of each stanza urging the members to "entwine the myrtle of Venus with Bacchus's vine." Bacchus, you may remember, was the Greek god of wine whose worship always seemed to inspire drunken orgies.

The notes were a little spread out — they covered more than an octave and a half — but the Englishmen had no trouble reaching them when they were half smashed. Other sets of words were written to fit the tune, some of them political satire and some rather racy.

The only reason you would ever know about Smith's tune . . . is that Francis Scott Key, in 1814, wrote his poem, "The Defense of Fort M'Henry," to fit it . . . he being somewhere around the eightieth person to use the melody.

The song has since, of course, become the United States national anthem, complete with all sorts of virtuous, moral, upright, patriotic overtones. The tune's past is completely forgotten by most. The line about Bacchus's vine has given way to ". . . o'er the land of the free and the home of the brave."

Which only goes to show that you can't judge a tune or a musical style by the words certain people attach to it, what they happen to be drinking while they sing it, etc., etc., etc.

In fact, most church members would be horrified if they knew that the tune for "O Sacred Head, Now Wounded," one of the most solemn, dignified hymns in the book, was originally a German jig! Some unknown writer in the 1500s put his lyrics to a common love song of the day.

And yet, it's not easy for some people to hold this distinction in the face of current rock music. Telling stories about past centuries is one thing, but applying the point of the stories to the present is quite another. If you were to interview even trained church musicians, you would find more than one who would mention "the devil's beat" — in other words, some certain type of rhythmic pattern which he considers intrinsically evil. If you pressed the issue and asked him to write out on a piece of musical score paper this "satanic" pattern which would supposedly lure any listener — European, Asian, African, American, anybody — toward evil, he might hesitate a bit. Because that theory has yet to be proved.

Granted, some American teen-agers use rock rhythms for some pretty sexy dancing, the kind of thing that belongs only in a married couple's bedroom. But what a copout to say, "The rhythm made me do it!" What about the floor, and the kids' shoes, and the Cheerios that gave them the energy? Are they also to blame? No way . . . the dancer himself is fully responsible for what he communicates through his motions. The music only makes things convenient for what he wants to express anyway.

Rock rhythms are used every day as, among other things, a simple expression of happiness by thousands of American teen-agers. The same beat, played in Iceland or Indonesia, would probably get strange stares, unless the listeners there had been preconditioned to accept the rock style.

Is there then nothing moral or immoral about the world of music? Doesn't it have anything to do with right and wrong?

You get into the heavy part when you leave the hemisphere of *impressions* (sounds) and get over into the other half (lyrics). Both moral and immoral people use the same bag of tricks to convey their messages. They work with the same instruments, the same chords, the same rhythms. But what they say in the words depends upon what's inside their heads — and that's where the difference lies.

When a Christian writes a set of words for a song, he's either talking about some aspect of knowing God or else something about God's world. He speaks from the point of view of someone who's in contact with the Creator. This doesn't mean he has a one-track mind, or that all his songs

George Harrison,
the Beatle most
enchanted with
Indian mysticism.

are "religious" songs. After all, when you write about God and His creation — you've included everything! The important thing is the perspective. As far as Bach was concerned, everything he wrote was "to the glory of God" — his church music, his concertos, his fugues, everything.

When a non-Christian writes a set of words for a song, he does it for any number of reasons — he feels creative, or he wants to make some money, or he has something he thinks is important to say, or he wants to play a joke on his listeners, or something else. His lack of relationship with God *may or may not* show through, depending on the topic.

For an example, go back to the Beatles' 1966 album, *Revolver*. George Harrison wrote and sang two songs on side one, "Taxman" and "Love You To." The first is a rather clever satire on the British version of the Internal Revenue Service, in which tax agents are painted as highway robbers:

If you drive a truck, I'll tax the street;
If you try to sit, I'll tax your seat;

If you get too cold, I'll tax the heat;
If you take a walk, I'll tax your feet.

Why? The only reason — and it's repeated over and over — "Cause I'm the taxman — yeah, I'm the taxman." The last line reminds you that "you're working for no one but me."

Nice, good-natured song. Probably even the British taxmen smiled about it.

But when Harrison shifts to the subject of love and sex, his playboy philosophy shows through. After describing a rather tentative relationship with a girl in which he doesn't get to spend much time with her, he recommends:

Make love all day long,
Make love singing songs.

There's people standing 'round,
They'll screw you in the ground,
They'll fill you in with all the sins, you'll see.

Harrison's answer to all these moralistic kill-joys? "I'll make love to you, if you want me to."

Five years later, in 1971, we got Harrison's confusion all in the same hit, "My Sweet Lord," which, incidentally, was Britain's top song for the year. He described his reaching out for some kind of faith: "I really want to know you, I really want to be with you." But who's "you"? It depended on which part of the song you listened to. At first the back-up voices sang "Hallelujah"; later on, it was "Hare Krishna." Take your choice, evidently.

It's right here where the people who object to rock make their strongest point: that the performers are often immoral people and they write very dirty songs.

That fact is quite true. Mick Jagger of the Rolling Stones is virtually the prototype for the sexy male singer. "Of course I do occasionally arouse primaeval instincts," he admits (the understatement of the decade) "but I mean, most men can do that. They can't do it to so many. I just happen to be able to do it to several thousand people. It's fun to do that. It's really just a game, isn't it? I mean these girls do it to themselves. They're all charged up. It's a dialogue of energy."

Many people quote Derek Taylor, one of the Beatles' early press officers, who told the *Saturday Evening Post:* "It's incredible, absolutely incredible. Here are these four boys from Liverpool. They're rude, they're profane, they're vulgar; and they've taken over the world. It's as if they'd founded a new religion."

Perhaps that's why John Lennon felt free to quip during a 1966 news conference: "The Beatles are more popular than Jesus." He wasn't ready for the uproar that he got; he was simply telling the unfortunate truth (in the mid-sixties, anyway) and assumed people would nod their heads.

Groups like Frank Zappa's Mothers of Invention have based entire careers on satire and put-on. Their vision of utopia in a song from the album *We're Only in It for the Money*: "There will come a time when you can even take your clothes off when you dance."

Paul Cantor of the Jefferson Airplane was clear about his group's intentions in a television interview: "Our music is intended to broaden the generation gap, to alienate children from their parents, and to prepare people for the revolution."

Yet you can't jump to the conclusion that all of rock is a master plot. The Beatles who were praising drugs and mysticism in 1967 had discarded both three years later. Not every rock star takes advantage of the groupies who wait for him after the evening's concert. In fact, who would you guess has been to bed with more chicks in his lifetime — the Doors' Jim Morrison or one of the older crooners? The only difference is that Morrison doesn't especially care who knows it, while the older pop stars don't flaunt it.

Have you ever listened closely to the lyrics of Frank Sinatra's 1966 song, "Strangers in the Night"? It just floats along so smoothly and says, "Who could know that we'd be making love before the night was through?" and goes right on and . . . what was that??

The truth is that immoral lyrics infect rock, pop, soul, country and western, Broadway . . . the entire spectrum. And they always have. For example, you can't get much more innocuous than *Kiss Me, Kate*, Cole Porter's musical comedy that opened on Broadway on December 30, 1948, took New York by storm and lasted for 1,077 performances. Since then, it must have been done by about every high school drama class in the country.

Or is *Kiss Me, Kate* so G-rated after all? About halfway through the play, a dressing room hand in the traveling stage company does a little ditty complaining about the hot Baltimore summer. It's just too sultry for much action with a local pickup. The third verse:

I'd like to fool with my baby tonight,
Break every rule with my baby tonight,
  (repeat)
But pillow, you'll be my baby tonight
'Cause it's too darn hot.

The problem has even been scientifically researched, he claims:

According to the Kinsey Report,
Every average man you know
Much prefers to play his favorite sport
When the temperature is low,
But when the thermometer goes way up

When Frank Sinatra got off the train in Pasadena, Calif., on August 11, 1943, the cops could hardly restrain the surging horde of teen-age fans.

> *And the weather is sizzlin' hot,*
> *Mr. Adam for his madam is not*
> *'Cause it's too darn hot.*

The verses get more explicit near the end:

> *I'd like to meet with my baby tonight,*
> *Get off my feet with my baby tonight,*
>   *(repeat)*
> *But no repeat with my baby tonight*
> *'Cause it's too darn hot.*

Match that one, Rolling Stones! (Admittedly, the Stones have tried.)

It all serves to illustrate that *everyone* within earshot of a radio, a television, or a stereo collection has a problem with immoral lyrics. The rock radio stations don't select their songs on the basis of Christian morality . . . but neither does Musak, the company that pipes background music into offices and shopping centers.

What are *we* — teenagers and adults — going to do about *our* problem?

The quick answer of some people, of course, is censoring. Let some responsible person throw out the objectionable songs before they get to the public. That gets rid of the real baddies . . . but doesn't do much about the more subtle ones. And music is a very subtle art. Peter, Paul and Mary once did a song called "I Dig Rock and Roll Music" which highlighted the fact that disc jockeys would turn down songs "unless I lay it between the lines."

Rock wasn't the first to lay it between the lines. Dropping little hints is what poetry is all about. "Too Darn Hot" never uses the words "sex" or "intercourse" or "impotence" — it doesn't have to. Everyone gets the message without it.

Other songs aren't even that explicit. In some ways, it's more accurate to talk about *dirty listeners* rather than *dirty lyrics*. When something isn't real bold, the people with dirty minds will pick it up faster than others. It's like the New Testament says, "To the pure all things are pure, but to the corrupt and unbelieving nothing is pure; their very minds and consciences are corrupted." (Titus 1:15)

We've all been around people who can make a dirty joke out of anything. They do the same with song lyrics; some lyrics are just easier for them to work with than others.

These complications are what drive the censors right up the wall. There were great outcries around 1966-67 when a lot of rock groups were fascinated with drugs and writing songs about it. Bob Dylan's "Mr. Tambourine Man," Donovan's "Mellow Yellow" and "Sunshine Superman," the Rolling Stones' "Something Happened to Me Yesterday," the Beatles' "Yellow Submarine," "Lucy in the Sky with Diamonds" and "A Day in the Life" were some of the suspects. The Jefferson Airplane's "White Rabbit" left little doubt.

But a lot of the others were far more subtle. What was a pro-drug song and what wasn't? It got to be a circus; even Peter Yarrow's fantasy song, "Puff, the Magic Dragon," was said to be about marijuana — which came as a great surprise to Yarrow!

There really is no easy answer. Each listener has to be his own censor — whether he's listening to the Top Forty station or the one with the World's Most Beautiful Music. If you sit down and listen to each for an hour and keep track of all the songs that justify taking advantage of other people (sexually, psychologically, economically) or have other moral statements that you can't agree with, you'll probably end up with about ten percent — *for each station*. Approximately half of the songs played will simply be love songs (or else heartbreak songs), because that has always been the favorite of popular songwriters.

The moral crisis in music, then, is not something you solve off in an RCA studio somewhere. The stars are going to compose and sing whatever

Frank Zappa,
who interprets almost
all of rock in terms
of sex and the
generation gap.

they like, and no one little record-buyer is going to stop them. Students in today's schools are not going to be able to avoid them.

The moral crisis is right inside individual heads, between the two ears. Some listeners, tragically, are sponges who silently soak up everything that's dished out as if it were coming directly from Gabriel himself, pure as snow. "Love You To" right along with "Taxman." "Strangers in the Night" as well as "Raindrops Keep Falling on My Head."

The entire hit-parade psychology exploits this type of person. If he doesn't own the number one record, he almost feels guilty! He has to run out and buy what's big (which thereby makes it a little bigger) and a snowball effect develops. Quantity becomes quality. The song or album is good because it's selling well, and it's selling well because it's good. The sponge-type person doesn't see anything hollow about that. He's caught

Iggy Stooge—
one fan magazine calls
him a "squirming demon"
who may leap out
into the crowd
to dance on top of
people's heads or
even rub peanut butter
all over his body
in the course of
the Stooges'
"private psychodrama."
What is the point—
music or theatrics?

up with the delusion that he's helping "make history" by his purchase.

The alert listener, in contrast, knows that he has to take care of his own head, regardless of whether a song rises or falls on the charts. He sets up a row of pigeonholes in his brain to sort the good stuff from the super-schlock. About twenty percent of the hits can be called "moral" — they make a strong, positive statement about values. At least sixty percent are "amoral" — they're about the flowers, the trees, or a million other things that simply exist; they're neither good or bad. Most romantic songs are so unspecific that they fall in this pigeonhole.

Then, the rest need to be tossed in the "immoral" bin — they definitely clash with Christian principles. If you're listening to the radio, about one song every half hour is this kind. The discriminating listener simply sorts the various songs as they come along, appreciating the good and rejecting the bad.

There's no way to insulate ourselves from every speck of dirt in music, even if we take Bob Larson's suggestion at the front of this chapter. We'll still pick it up in a dozen different places, simply because we live in a world that is not yet godly — not by a long shot.

There are probably about as many filthy books around today as there are filthy songs. But few people are advocating a ban on reading! Likewise, television is a constant mixture of good and bad, moral and immoral, enlightening and cruddy. The only solution is an invisible strainer in the brain of the viewer. And if the schlock gets piled high enough, it's time to switch stations.

Perhaps the best guideline comes from St. Paul, who advised: "If you believe in goodness and if you value the approval of God, fix your minds on whatever is true and honorable and just and pure and lovely and praiseworthy." (Phil. 4:8, Modern English New Testament) There's a difference between being aware of dirty music, and wallowing in it.

We must be the housekeepers of our own minds. The listener who is too lazy to do his chores is asking for trouble and a polluted mind. We have to pitch the garbage we don't want right back out the door.

CHAPTER FOUR

64

Ecstasy, bliss,
surprise, glee,
joy, celebration,
excitement, gusto,
wonder, awe . . .

. . . solitude, fear,
tension, hesitation,
uncertainty, mistrust,
boredom, loneliness,
meditation, fatigue,
reflection . . .

experience,
feeling,
impression,
discovery,
newness,
perception

—these are
the alphabet of music!

THE EARLY DAYS OF FREEDOM

Religion and rock — they've been enemies most of the time. Clergymen have raged against the "new barbarians," and rock groups, from the Beatles in "Eleanor Rigby" on up, have returned the vitriol. The church, they said in a dozen different ways, was against fun, self-expression and rhythm.

But the last few years have seen something of a cease-fire, at least in some areas. Rock musicians have rediscovered that Jesus Himself was an intense, purposeful firebrand, not a meek-and-mild relic. And some church people have gone back to reread parts of their Bible. There they've found ordinary people expressing the full range of life's agonies and ecstasies — joy, pain, loneliness, triumph, sorrow, reflection — through music.

The Bible's songs were often far from formal — the pouring out of common folk feelings, exactly as the people felt them. In fact, it all seems to have started thousands of years ago with Jubal. . . .

You don't remember who Jubal was? That's O.K. . . . he lived too long ago to have much written about him. In fact, his only claim to fame is that "he was the father of all those who play the lyre and pipe," according to Genesis.

Actually, he got his musical talent from his father, Lamech. Lamech was a pretty impulsive man, evidently the world's first polygamist. He also committed, so far as we know, the second murder in history. A teen-ager jumped him one day, and in self-defense Lamech whipped out his knife or picked up a nearby rock or some other weapon and killed him.

That night around the fire, he told his wives what had happened. It was no ordinary story; Lamech made it into a chant, complete with the rationalization that he was no worse than his ancestor Cain, who had murdered in cold blood.

Adah and Zillah, hear my voice;
You wives of Lamech, hearken to what I say:

I have slain a man for wounding me,
A young man for striking me.

If Cain is avenged sevenfold,
Truly Lamech seventy-sevenfold.[1]

Jubal listened in silence. His older brother, Jabal, was far more interested in cattle and farming, the Bible says. Their half-brother, Tubal-cain, was fascinated with forging metal. Jubal alone heard the sounds of music and tried to create his own from camel-gut strings on a handmade lyre (forerunner of the guitar) and from flutes made from the shin bones of cattle. His name is echoed today in English words such as *jubilant* and *jubilee.*

Those were the centuries before music became so stiff and formal, when people made up their own songs or chants to celebrate the big events of their lives. They didn't label it "sacred" or "secular" — they simply sang of God in the midst of life. Visualize what it must have been like:

SCENE ONE: THE RED SEA FESTIVAL. It's the morning after. Moses and over a million Hebrews had been up all night, nervously eyeing the Egyptian battalions, who had decided to wait for daylight before swooping in for the capture. The morning sun has now begun to rise behind their backs, casting long shadows across the water. The waves have stopped thrashing, and the desperate shouts of drowning men and the high-pitched neighs of panicky horses are gone. Here and there, corpses are floating toward the beach.

Moses and his newly born nation are exhausted. Physically, they have moved themselves and all their belongings across a narrow channel bed in the darkness, not knowing what happened to the water and afraid to stop and investigate. Emotionally, they can hardly believe that there in the sea are the oppressors — dead. The crowd is quiet, stunned, only slowly grasping the fact that there is no more Egyptian military machine to bully them. *Free at last!*

Moses can't think of anything to do but celebrate. His weather-beaten voice begins to sing . . . he's making up the words as he goes:

I will sing to the Lord,
For he has triumphed gloriously;
He has thrown both horse and rider into the sea.

It sounds good. He repeats the lines, smoothing out the melody this time, and the crowd begins to hum along with him.

He sings it again, and now the people are picking it up. Then he branches off:

The Lord is my strength, my song, and my salvation.
He is my God, and I will praise him.
He is my father's God — I will exalt him.
The Lord is a warrior —
Yes, Jehovah is his name.

Over and over, with more people joining all the time. Moses smiles in relief from the night's tension; the mood gradually changes to exuberance.

He has overthrown Pharaoh's chariots and armies,
Drowning them in the sea.
The famous Egyptian captains are dead beneath the waves.

The water covers them.
They went down into the depths like a stone.

Your right hand, O Lord, is glorious in power;
It dashes the enemy to pieces.
In the greatness of your majesty
You overthrew all those who rose against you.
You sent forth your anger, and it consumed them as fire
    consumes straw.

At the blast of your breath
The waters divided!
They stood as solid walls to hold the seas apart.

The enemy said, "I will chase after them,
Catch up with them, destroy them.
I will cut them apart with my sword
And divide the captured booty."

But God blew with his wind, and the sea covered them.
They sank as lead in the mighty waters.

The roar of the crowd is loud now, and not everyone is singing the same lines. Snatches are passed from one section to the next — the effect

Miriam leading
the Red Sea
Festival,
as pictured
by Artist
Jennie Wylie.

is like a huge round with about ten parts going at once. And there's more
to come —

Who else is like the Lord among the gods?
Who is glorious in holiness like him?
Who is so awesome in splendor,
A wonder-working God?
You reached out your hand and the earth swallowed them.

You have led the people you redeemed.
But in your lovingkindness

You have guided them wonderfully
To your holy land.

The nations heard what happened, and they trembled.
Fear has gripped the people of Philistia.
The leaders of Edom are appalled,
The mighty men of Moab tremble:
All the people of Canaan melt with fear.
Terror and dread have overcome them.

O Lord, because of your great power they won't attack us!
Your people whom you purchased
Will pass by them in safety.
You will bring them in and plant them on your mountain,
Your own homeland, Lord —
The sanctuary you made for them to live in.
Jehovah shall reign forever and forever.

The first lines keep coming back . . . by this time Miriam, Moses' sister, has unpacked a tambourine and added a vigorous beat. Other women do the same, and before long they're dancing in huge circles, beating and singing for all they're worth:

Sing to the Lord, for he has triumphed gloriously.
The horse and rider have been drowned in the sea![2]

SCENE TWO: A NEW MOTHER'S ECSTASY. A woman in her thirties lies sobbing on the floor of the Tabernacle as evening falls in Shiloh. The daytime crowds are gone, and she sheds a bit of her self-consciousness as she pleads with Jehovah, "O Lord of heaven, if you will look down upon my sorrow and answer my prayer and give me a son . . . then I will give him back to you . . . and he'll be yours for his entire lifetime. . . ." She is desperate; the sarcasm and sneers of her rival, Peninnah, who shares her husband's affections, have driven her to the brink of insanity.

An aged priest sits dozing on his special chair beside the entrance. He notices the prostrate figure in the twilight. The mouth is moving . . . but Eli hears nothing. "She's drunk!" he thinks to himself. "Must you come here drunk?" he calls out with agitation. "Throw away your bottle."

The woman jerks up, and wipes her eyes quickly. "Oh, no, sir! I'm not drunk! But I am very sad and I was pouring out my heart to the Lord," she explains. "Please don't think that I am just some drunken bum!"

The priest relaxes. "In that case," he says, "cheer up! May the Lord of Israel grant you your petition, whatever it is!"

74

Hannah's
return trip,
as painted by
F. W. W. Topham
in the 1800s.

The woman gets to her feet, obviously relieved. She has heard the encouragement of God's representative, and somehow, some way, she will have a child.

Three months later, Hannah has a strange smile on her face. She knows she is pregnant. Elkanah, her husband, is thrilled; Peninnah and her brood of rowdy children are forced into silence. Before the next annual trip to Shiloh, she cradles a baby son. His name is Samuel; it means "asked of God."

Hannah skips the Shiloh trip this year; she's waiting until her son is old enough to be left there with Eli. Eventually, the day comes, and a wave of nostalgia sweeps over her as she walks, toddler in hand, into the Tabernacle once again. The same dirt floor . . . the same roof of skins . . . the same holy golden furniture. Her heart is beating wildly; she absolutely *must* sing!

How I rejoice in the Lord!
How he has blessed me!

Now I have an answer for my enemies,
For the Lord has solved my problem.
How I rejoice!
No one is as holy as the Lord!
There is no other God,
Nor any Rock like our God.

Peninnah can hear her, of course, but Hannah couldn't care less. In fact, she begins bending her words in Peninnah's direction:

Quit acting so proud and arrogant!
The Lord knows what you have done,
And he will judge your deeds. . . .

The Lord kills,
The Lord gives life.
Some he causes to be poor
And others to be rich.
He cuts one down
And lifts another up.
He lifts the poor from the dust —
Yes, from a pile of ashes —
And treats them as princes
Sitting in the seats of honor,
For all the earth is the Lord's
And he has set the world in order. . . .[3]

SCENE THREE: CONCERTS OF TERROR. The monarch paces the hallway; it's late at night. He suddenly whirls to look behind him, his eyes flashing with fear. "What was that?" he shouts.

"Nothing, your majesty," his valet replies. "Nothing at all. There was no sound."

The king's hulking frame shudders, and he continues down the hall. He has not slept more than an hour at a time for the past week; he hears voices, he is gripped by illusions of plots against his life, he mistrusts any smile or pleasantry from his aides. Finally, he slumps to the floor, and his eyes close; the valet is grateful for a moment of rest, and tiptoes away.

Late the next afternoon, as the king finishes business and prepares to leave his throne room, a young man is ushered in. An assistant introduces him: his name is David, the eighth and youngest son of a Bethlehem farmer named Jesse. According to Secret Service, he is not only courageous, a good prospect for a soldier, but also fairly accomplished on the lyre.

76

Stop the music!

That night, David provides background music for the king's dinner hour, soft tunes he has up to now played only for grazing sheep and family members. The king is impressed; he sings along on songs he knows, and that night gets quickly to sleep without trouble.

*   *   *

Months have passed, and David is no longer the shepherd-boy prodigy. Overnight he has become a national hero through his audacious attack on the archenemy Goliath. King Saul boasts about him at every public appearance and has made him his armor carrier.

But music — the great bond which had welded the two together in the first place — is now turned to drive a wedge between them. As they march victoriously in a military parade, the crowds begin to chant a loaded ditty:

Saul has slain his thousands,
And David his ten thousands.

The king suddenly clams up, and that night he is tortured by ugly fantasies again.

The next day, David sits playing his lyre, trying to calm the brilliant but bedeviled ruler. Saul begins raging about the room . . . he chooses a spear from the wall rack . . . he stares at its tip, mumbling even while David plucks the strings. . . .

Suddenly, a glint of metal flying through the air! David hits the floor, dropping his lyre as he falls . . . the spear goes *thwack!* into the paneled wall above his chair.

Less than a week later, the same thing happens again. The honeymoon is over; David is demoted to a minor officer's rank. When Saul wants him to marry his daughter, David smells entrapment, but complies. Only the kind words of his friends keep him in Jerusalem.

*   *   *

The latest rumors have it that Saul wants to forget the past and welcome his son-in-law back. Perhaps David's latest victory over the Philistines has something to do with it; then again, perhaps the king has had a change of heart. David begins spending time at the palace once again, and Saul is congenial.

One day, the old telltale signs — fidgeting, incoherence, anger — begin to show as Saul plunges into another seizure. He calls for musical therapy once again. David obliges . . . but keeps his eyes up, his fingers playing blind on the strings . . . the king fumbles with his spear . . . it's all so familiar . . . *swish!* here it comes — and David is out of the room for good. Out of the capital city, out into the countryside. At least, people there don't try to kill you for doing them favors.

*   *   *

And yet, over the next months and years, David learns that the king still has many loyal subjects. The locals will not attack him outright, but they do persist in tipping off Saul's F.B.I. whenever they see him.

David runs to Philistine territory briefly, then returns to hide out in a cave near Adullam. The word spreads that he's back, and each day a trickle of men come to join his guerrilla band, eventually around 400 of them.

It's a time of apprehension, of uncertainty, of weariness. The tension inevitably finds words in one of David's seventy-three songs:

Be merciful to me, O God,
Be merciful to me,
For in thee my soul takes refuge;
In the shadow of thy wings I will take refuge,
Till the storms of destruction pass by.

I cry to God Most High,
To God who fulfills his purpose for me.
He will send from heaven and save me,
He will put to shame those who trample upon me.
God will send forth his steadfast love and his faithfulness!

I lie in the midst of lions
That greedily devour the sons of men;
Their teeth are spears and arrows,
Their tongues sharp swords.

(Chorus) *Be exalted, O God, above the heavens!*
            Let thy glory be over all the earth!

They set a net for my steps;
My soul was bowed down.
They dug a pit in my way,
But they have fallen into it themselves.

My heart is steadfast, O God,
My heart is steadfast!
I will sing and make melody!
Awake, my soul!
Awake, O harp and lyre!
I will awake the dawn!

I will give thanks to thee, O Lord,
Among the peoples;
I will sing praises to thee
Among the nations.

For thy steadfast love is great to the heavens,
Thy faithfulness to the clouds.
(repeat chorus)[4]

SCENE FOUR: A DRAMATIC MEAL. Thirteen men are stretched out on mats and couches in an upstairs room, eating a supper of roast lamb and flat, tough bread.

The meal is special, because it is the Passover season. Across Jerusalem that day at the Temple, a lamb has been killed in sacrifice, its blood sprinkled according to ceremony, commemorating the exodus of Israel from Egypt. All across the city, families or informal groups such as these men are meeting for the ritual meal.

The conversation runs from one topic to another, from the congestion of the city at this holiday time to the kindness of the homeowner who has loaned them the room and utensils for the evening. Suddenly the man in the seamless robe, the leader of the group, interrupts: "One of you will betray me."

The room gets deathly quiet. What had He said? Who would do something like that — after all they'd been through together?

The others know better than to mock the idea. He's been dropping hints for weeks now. And if Jesus knows He's going to be betrayed by one of the men in the room . . . He obviously knows which one.

"Am I the one?" Everybody has the same question.

"It is the one I honor by giving the bread dipped in the sauce," He says, handing it to Judas Iscariot.

Judas eats it and says nothing. The room is electrified. Jesus breaks the silence. "Hurry — do it now." Judas quickly gets up and heads down the stairs, out onto the street. The others don't know what to think.[5]

Then comes the sharing of another loaf of flat bread; Jesus says it is symbolic of His "broken body." The cup of wine is passed around; Jesus says it represents His blood. The eleven minds are swirling with puzzles, overridden by a fear of the next few hours.

Jesus talks for a long time this evening, and then just before they leave, there is one last Passover tradition to carry out: the singing of the last half of the Hallel (Psalms 115-118). Some of the lines are poignant:

. . . The snares of death encompassed me;
The pangs of Sheol laid hold on me:
I suffered distress and anguish.
Then I called on the name of the Lord:
"O Lord, I beseech thee, save my life!"

. . . What shall I render to the Lord

80

For all his bounty to me?
I will lift up the cup of salvation
And call on the name of the Lord,
I will pay my vows to the Lord
In the presence of all his people.
Precious in the sight of the Lord
Is the death of his saints.

. . . Out of my distress I called on the Lord;
The Lord answered me and set me free.
With the Lord on my side I do not fear.
What can man do to me?
The Lord is on my side to help me;
I shall look in triumph on those who hate me.

. . . The stone which the builders rejected
Has become the head of the corner.
This is the Lord's doing,
It is marvelous in our eyes.

Only one man of the twelve really knows what he's singing, and how soon its shocking reality will hit. They blow out the lamps, descend the stairs, and head for Gethsemane. . . .

SCENE FIVE: THE JAILBREAK. The crowd is buzzing, milling around, asking each other what about the two men up there on the witness stand. A cluster of merchants is shouting something about illegal activities, interference with commerce, but no one, including the Philippian judges, appears to know what to do.

The judges finally decide on investigation by torture. The two visitors are ordered stripped to the waist and then beaten with wooden whips. As the soldiers begin their work, Paul worries about whether Silas can stand this. He himself has been through it before, at the hands of hysterical Jews in Asia Minor . . . but the Romans can be superbly sadistic when they want to be.

The rods very quickly raise welts and then begin to splatter blood. Silas remains conscious, as does Paul, but neither spill out any more information than that they had simply freed a girl from demons by the power of Jesus Christ. There is nothing else to tell. The merchants insist again that the pair are dangerous subversives, a threat to the emperor himself.

Almost before Paul realizes it, he is being hustled off to jail for the first (although not the last) time in his life. "They can't do this!" he says to himself, and begins to demand a full trial on the basis of his Roman citizenship, but no one will listen. He and Silas are kicked down a dingy staircase to maximum security — the lowest dungeon in the building. The soldiers threaten the jailer with death if there's a jailbreak . . . he returns to clamp the two prisoners' ankles into pinching stocks. Sitting on the floor, with no support for their gouged backs, they wait for their eyes to adjust to the darkness. Shadowy figures gradually come into focus . . . the air is filled with curses of welcome.

Paul's mind turns back to a few weeks before . . . the night in Troas when he had the vision. A Macedonian welcoming him, pleading with him, "Come over here and help us." Where was that man? Where were any Macedonians like him? Had it been an illusion? Or had God indeed spoken to him in the night?

As the evening wears on, the pain in their backs is replaced by deep-down aches from sitting in their extended positions. But their minds are not on their suffering. They're talking about Lydia, the Asian fabric seller who responded to the Gospel last week. They're talking about the teen-age girl who is no longer tormented by demons.

It's close to midnight. Paul reminds Silas of the time he visited Jerusalem eight or nine years ago. Silas was living there then . . . and Peter had been arrested by Herod. They reminisce about the all-night prayer meetings in people's homes . . . and the miracle of Peter's release from prison!

They begin to pray — out loud — for a similar miracle tonight. Why not? God is still God; they need to be free to carry the Good News on. Paul begins to sing, what words or tune we don't know . . . perhaps something of trust and hope from the Old Testament, perhaps something fresh on the spot. Silas joins him, louder now. The other prisoners listen respectfully to these two unbelievable newcomers.

On and on they sing. And all of a sudden, the place begins to rumble . . . !⁶

FINALE: The final scenes of music in the Bible are harder to imagine. They were seen by only one man — John — in his revelation from exile. He was, for a few hours, a visitor in heaven. At least eight times he was flooded with the mighty cascading reverberations of celestial choirs:
Holy, holy, holy, is the Lord God Almighty,
*Who was and is and is to come!*⁷

Worthy art thou, our Lord and God,
To receive glory and honor and power,

For thou didst create all things,
And by thy will they existed and were created.[8]

Hallelujah!
Salvation and glory and power belong to our God,
For his judgments are true and just. . . .
Hallelujah!
For the Lord our God the Almighty reigns.
Let us rejoice and exult and give him the glory. . . .[9]
    To get the full effect . . . we'll have to hear it for ourselves.

[1] Gen. 4:23.24 — Revised Standard Version
[2] Exodus 15 — Living Bible
[3] I Samuel 1. 2 — Living Bible
[4] Psalm 57 — Revised Standard Version
[5] Matt. 26:17-22: John 13:26-28 — Living Bible
[6] Acts 16 — King James Version
[7] Revelation 4:8 — Revised Standard Version
[8] Revelation 4:11 — Revised Standard Version
[9] Rev. 19:1.2.6.7 — Revised Standard Version

The verve and excitement has been gutted from the structures of Christianity only too often. Rules and systems, made by sincere people to preserve what they considered the finest in worship music, have turned out to be suffocating.

Slowly the structures crumble . . . and life springs up

beside them once again.

And
vitality
is
reborn!

"WHO DO YOU THINK YOU ARE – KING DAVID?"

The days of free expression lasted a couple of centuries past New Testament times before the Church began getting sticky about music. Clement of Alexandria, about a hundred years after John's vision, wrote to a friend: "We cultivate our fields, praising; we sail the seas, hymning; our lives are filled with prayers and praises and Scripture readings, before meals and before bed, and even during the night. By this means we unite ourselves to the Heavenly choir."

Josephus, the historian, claimed that Christians facing death in the Roman Coliseum could be heard singing above the roar of the lions and the shouts of the bloodthirsty crowd. Tertullian describes a meeting of Christians in North Africa around 200 A.D.: "We have plenty of songs, verses, sentences and proverbs. After hand-washing, and the bringing of lights, each is asked to stand forth and sing, as he can, a hymn to God, either one of the Holy Scriptures or one of his own composing."

Tertullian doesn't say what they did with monotones or introverts!

Then, the problems began — problems of tightening up, regimentation, which have plagued Christians right up to the present. By the fourth century, the Church was locked in great battles over doctrine, and the heretics were busily writing hymns to spread their ideas. The Gnostics wrote an entire collection of psalms; the biggest problem was with the Arians, who sent singing teams out into villages to propagate their doctrine that Christ was not fully God, but only a person whom God the Father had created at some point in time.

Free, spontaneous God-music almost went down the drain because of it. A synod at Laodicea in 363 A.D. voted to ban all music except David's psalms from then on. Furthermore, laymen were to shut up; only "regularly appointed singers . . . shall sing in the Church." That kept Arian ideas out of church music — except where Arians had the votes to appoint the singers and control entire congregations.

The man who reversed the tide was, strangely enough, a Roman governor in the north Italian city of Milan. Ambrose was from a ruling family, became a lawyer, then a judge, worked his way up the bureaucracy and was put in charge of the province of Aemilia-Liguria in 370. Four years later, the local bishop, Auxentius, died, and it looked as if it would be a stormy contest to decide his successor. The people of Milan suddenly had an idea: why not choose their governor? Ambrose went from a unbaptized layman to a bishop in eight days!

And although he didn't know a lot of theology, he knew that he liked the kind of plain song, or chant melody, Auxentius had introduced into the services. The new bishop began to write hymns, encouraged others to do so, and made an attempt at a notation system for his music. In his writings, he mentions "the great bond of unity when all the people raise their voices in one chorus."

The next year, Valentinian II was named emperor, a mere four-year-old boy. His mother, Justina, who was an enthusiastic Arian, ran the empire for him. Finally, in 384 or 385 A.D., she demanded that Ambrose surrender the basilica in Milan to the Arians and sent her armies to enforce her order.

Ambrose could not bring himself to give in to those who would deny Christ's divinity. He gathered his congregation inside the basilica to resist. The soldiers hesitated outside; for several days and nights, neither side moved. To pass the time, Ambrose taught his people to sing psalms "in the oriental manner," as he wrote later, meaning as the Syrian churches sang, with two choirs singing to each other, alternating back and forth. Ambrose changed it slightly, so that he sang the beginning lines, and the congregation answered with a simple response. In his mind he told himself, "If they keep busy singing, they will not wax faint through the tediousness of sorrow."

His courage paid off; the empress-mother Justina backed down. The new style of music soon spread to surrounding churches, and laymen were once again singing in worship, instead of merely listening to professionals.

Only a few months later, a visiting teacher from North Africa attended a service in the Milan church. He was a pagan, and a rather vulgar one at that; his name was Augustine. Ambrose was the first Christian intellectual he had ever heard, and the church's music overwhelmed him. Later on, he wrote in his *Confessions,* "How abundantly did I weep to hear those hymns and canticles of thine, being touched to the very quick by the voice of the sweet Church song. . . .

"Those sounds flowed into my ears, and the truth streamed into my heart; so that my feelings of devotion overflowed, and the tears ran from my eyes, and I was happy in them.

"It was only a little while before," Augustine continued, "that the church in Milan had begun to practice this kind of consolation and exultation . . . singing psalms and hymns after the manner of the Eastern churches. . . . The custom has been retained from that day to this and has been imitated by man, indeed, in almost all congregations throughout the world."

Augustine became a believer and was baptized there; he went on to become the bishop of Hippo in North Africa, and the greatest thinker of the ancient Church. As for Ambrose, the music he reinstated lasted for two hundred years, until Pope Gregory wanted to "displace the melodious style of music of Ambrose with a more stately and solemn monotone." The people of Milan were not impressed with the new Gregorian chant. To this day, *seventeen centuries later,* the Ambrosian chant is used in the Catholic diocese of Milan and as far north as nearby Switzerland.

Eleven hundred years later, Martin Luther, of course, rocked the Church so hard with his preaching that the new music he promoted was simply part of the same explosion. His hymns rushed into a vacuum; the German people had for centuries listened only to the clergy when they went to church, and the majority of Christian songs available were addressed to the Virgin Mary or other saints, not to God. Meanwhile, the *Minnesingers* — German folk musicians who traveled and sang mainly about love and beauty — had given the people something to hum. Luther was smart enough to grab some of their tunes and add Christian words.

"His songs have damned more souls than all his books and speeches," cried some Catholics. "The whole people is singing itself into the Lutheran doctrine."

To keep them singing, Luther, who had a strong tenor voice and played both the flute and the lute (a pear-shaped guitar), turned out four different hymn collections during his lifetime. The first one, including four hymns of his own, came in 1524, and it was a *Sacred Song-book for Three, Four or Five Voices* — a big innovation for his time. After all, the Church was not quite ready to approve "polyphony" (singing in parts), as it was called, but Luther was excited about it. "Therein one may see the boundless love of God, who gave to man this power," he wrote. "Nothing

Maverick Martin Luther (Niall MacGinnis) in the biographical movie.

is so strange and wonderful as a simple tune accompanied by three, four, or five other voices which gambol about and ornament it in many ways."

He wrote thirty-six songs, including "A Mighty Fortress Is Our God" and possibly "Away in a Manger." Some were paraphrases of psalms or other Scriptures, but others were entirely original. He wrote up to thirteen of the tunes as well. Along with his sermons and treatises, his hymn publishing kept four printers constantly busy. Students peddled his literature around the country, even though in some parts of Germany possession of a Luther hymnbook meant prison or death.

His last collection came out in 1545, a year before his death, and had 101 songs which were widely distributed. His preface read: "What I wish, is to make hymns for the people, that the Word of God may dwell in their hearts by means of song also." By that time, his wish had already come true. To anyone who objected to his techniques, he had a ready comeback: "Why should the devil have all the good tunes?"

His fellow reformers John Calvin and John Knox were not quite that freewheeling, however. In Calvin's Geneva, "humanly composed" hymns were banned, and only David's psalms were allowed. Christians thus put themselves right back in the same box as over a thousand years before. Louis Bourgeois, a friend of Calvin's, wrote the familiar "Doxology," a paraphrase of a psalm. A few years later he got himself in trouble by changing his own tune — *without permission* — and wound up in jail! When Bourgeois tried part-singing with the church choir, he was quickly driven out of town.

All through the rest of the sixteenth and seventeenth centuries, Protestants outside Germany were busy squeezing, editing and reworking the psalms to sound like Renaissance poetry. "When we have searched around, here and there, we shall find none better, or more suitable, than the Psalms of David which the Holy Spirit dictated," wrote Calvin.

Somewhere around 1690, a young English teen-ager wasn't so sure about that. His name was Isaac Watts, and he was frankly bored to death by the psalm-singing in his church. To oppose the status quo was nothing unusual in his family; they already were part of the Nonconformist (Congregational) group which had broken with the Church of England. As a matter of fact, his father had been serving a year-long jail sentence for his beliefs at the time of Isaac's birth.

So one day, somewhere between the ages of sixteen and twenty, the boy let his father know what he thought of the psalms they sang at church.

His dad was unimpressed. "Those psalms were good enough for your grandfather and for me, and they will serve you just as well."

Isaac stuck to his opinion.

"Well, if you could make any better hymns, why don't you try?" his father shot back.

"All right, I will," he said. He promptly went to his room, opened his Bible to the Book of Revelation, read the praises offered to Christ in chapter five, and then wrote his first hymn, "Behold the Glories of the Lamb."

He took it back downstairs and showed it to his father, who was forthright enough to have it sung the next Sunday morning in church. Evidently some of the other churchgoers were also getting tired of rehashed psalms, for Isaac was asked to write another hymn for next week. He kept that pace up for the next two years!

The lyrics were prickly at times. His first collection, *Hymns and Sacred Songs* (1707) included "We're Marching to Zion." Modern hymnals almost always leave out Watts' second verse:

The sorrows of the mind,
Be banished from the place,
Religion never was designed
To make our pleasure less.

The book also included "When I Survey the Wondrous Cross" and "At the Cross."

A doctor in town offered to pay his way to become an Anglican minister, but he turned it down, preferring "to take my lot with the dissenters." After four years of study, he became a tutor, then pastor of a London chapel in 1702. The one thing he couldn't accomplish was finding a wife. He was extremely short — not much more than five feet — and frail, and his proposal to a young woman was turned down.

The church, however, grew so fast it had to relocate twice during the next ten years. But that time, Watts' health was breaking, and a wealthy couple in the church, Sir Thomas and Lady Abney, invited him to spend a week's vacation at their country home. The thirty-eight-year-old bachelor ended up staying there the rest of his life, coming back to London to preach only when he felt well enough. The rest of the time he wrote books and about 600 hymn lyrics in all. He complained about the lack of good tunes, but not being a musician, there was nothing he could do about it.

He got back to tradition in 1719 with *The Psalms of David Imitated in the Language of the New Testament* — but David would hardly recognize them. In the collection were "Joy to the World" (his version of Psalm 98), "Jesus Shall Reign Where'er the Sun" (from Psalm 72) and "O God, Our Help in Ages Past" (from Psalm 90). The way he saw it, "Some of the Psalms are almost opposite to the spirit of the gospel; many of them are foreign to New Testament principles and widely different to the present circumstances of Christians. If we are to make Christian hymns of the Psalms, we must first rewrite them in the way that David would have written them if he had been an eighteenth-century Christian instead of an Old Testament Jew." David no longer being around, Watts simply decided to help him out.

By the time Watts died, another Englishman was already whipping out hymns at the rate of one or more a day. Charles Wesley, younger brother of John Wesley, the founder of Methodism, had a mind that could write poetry on the street corner, in church, on horseback, in the fields, almost anywhere, without being distracted. In fifty years he wrote approximately *6,500* hymns for a total of *180,000* lines of verse!

He tried them out, of course, at the end of each of his brother John's sermons, when he was expected to have a new song ready. Like Watts, he didn't write tunes (he didn't have time!); "it was Wesley's practice to seize upon any song of the theater or the street, the moment it became popular, and make it carry some newly written hymn into the homes of the people," says hymnographer Silas H. Paine. He picked up some of Handel's classical melodies and got criticized for being too "worldly." He even had the nerve to use England's new national anthem, "God Save the

Charles Wesley—
he even made a
hymn out of the
national anthem.

King" (the one Americans use for "My Country, 'Tis of Thee"). Wesley's version: "Come Thou Almighty King." Only later was it matched with the Italian tune used today.

Hymn-writing was simply Charles Wesley's main medium for expressing his faith. Two days after his conversion on May 21, 1738, lying sick in bed, he wrote his first one:

Where shall my wond'ring Soul begin?
How shall I All to Heaven aspire?
A slave redeem'd from Death and Sin,
A brand pluck'd from Eternal Fire,
How shall I equal Triumphs raise,
Or sing my great Deliverer's Praise?

The next day, his brother John felt his "heart strangely warmed" as he sat in church listening to the reading of Luther's writings on Romans. Though both were ordained priests in the Church of England and had even served as missionaries to the Indians in Georgia, only now did they begin to preach with conviction.

Exactly a year later, to commemorate his new faith, Charles wrote "O

For a Thousand Tongues," which has been page one in the *Methodist Hymn Book* since 1780. Within two years, he had written "Jesus, Lover of My Soul" — but John thought this one was too sentimental. It was missing from all Methodist hymnals until nine years after Charles' death.

Some of his others weren't really so great, but out of 6,500 tries, a few losers should be expected. One time he sang this one for an audience of tough coal miners:

Ye liars and blasphemers too,
  Who speak the phrase of hell,
Ye murderers all, He died for you,
  He loved your soul so well.

Presumable, Wesley wasn't quite so stinging the day he, at the age of forty-two, was married to Sarah Gwynne. His diary reads: "I rose at four, spent three and one-half hours in prayer or singing with my brother and Sally [Sarah] and Beck. At eight I led my Sally to church . . . my brother joined our hands. It was a most solemn season of love. Never had I more of the Divine presence at the sacrament. My brother gave out a hymn. He then prayed over us in strong faith. We walked back to the house and joined again in prayer. Prayer and thanksgiving was our whole employment."

His hymns covered Christmas ("Hark, the Herald Angels Sing"), Calvary ("And Can It Be that I Should Gain?"), Easter ("Christ the Lord Is Risen Today"), responsibility ("A Charge to Keep Have I"), love ("Love Divine, All Loves Excelling," which was a takeoff from John Dryden's popular "Fairest Isle, all Isles Excelling") and just about every other topic he could think of. His music was the natural product of his life with Christ; you can sense his frustration as he writes in his journal, "Near Ripley my horse threw and fell on me . . . my companion thought I had broken my neck. But my leg only was bruised, my hand sprained, and my head stunned, which spoiled my making hymns till the next day."

With the momentum of Watts and Wesley, one would think that church music would never bog down again. But in America during the Revolutionary period as well as the early 1800s, Christians renewed the same old hassles as in previous centuries: modern song-writers, or psalms only? Choirs or no choirs? Instruments or no instruments?

One elderly Presbyterian minister was invited to preach in a church which had recently installed an organ. When he was called upon to pray, he snapped, "Call on the machine! If it can sing and play to the glory of God, it can pray to the glory of God also. Call on the machine!"

The hymns of Watts and Wesley became standardized; what more was needed? (The only alteration was, after 1776, to edit out some of the complimentary references to the British king and empire!) In fact, the hell-fire-and-brimstone outlook of the Puritans made them lean toward hymns of judgment; early American hymnals left out "Jesus, Lover of My Soul" but included another one Wesley wrote about death:

Ah, lovely appearance of death!
What sight upon earth is so fair?
Not all the pageants that breathe
Can with a dead body compare.
With solemn delight I survey
The corpse, when the spirit is fled,
In love with the beautiful clay,
And longing to lie in its stead.

Some worried soul even wrote a feverish ballad called "Wicked Polly" as a warning to teenagers:

O young people, hark while I relate
The story of poor Polly's fate.
She was a lady young and fair
Who died a-groaning in despair.
She'd go to balls, and dance and play
In spite of all her friends might say.
One Sabbath morning she fell sick,
Her stubborn heart began to ache.
She called her mother to her bed,
Her eyes were rolling in her head.
"My loving mother, you I leave,
For wicked Polly do not grieve,
For I must burn forevermore.
When thousand thousand years are o'er,
When I am dead remember well
Your wicked Polly groans in hell."
She wrung her hands, and groaned and cried,
And gnawed her tongue before she died;
Her nails turned black, her voice did fail,
She died, and left this lower vail.
May this a warning be to those
That love the ways that Polly chose.

Around the middle of the 1800s, things began to turn. The Sunday school movement was gaining speed, and simple songs were written by Americans to help children learn. A new kind of music, the "gospel song," was born, addressed not to God but to the other listeners as a form of testimony.

And as you might guess, some people defended hymns and fought gospel songs exactly as their fathers had defended psalms and fought hymns!

Ira D. Sankey with the beloved, blind hymn-writer Fanny Crosby.

One man who took much of the brunt of this was Ira D. Sankey, song-leader for the famous D. L. Moody. He didn't write a lot of songs, but he dug them out from other people and made them popular in Moody's meetings. Moody was absolutely tone-deaf (his daughter-in-law once tricked him by playing "Yankee Doodle" slowly with soulful chords after he had asked for "Rock of Ages," and Moody never knew the difference!). But he could see the power of music on an audience. Sankey had led the fight to get an organ installed in his home church in New Castle, Pa., loved music and was quickly talked out of a civil service job to come with the Chicago evangelist.

The late 1800s weren't exactly the most outstanding period in music; it was the age of Stephen Foster, Civil War songs, and tinkling Victorian tunes. Thus, Sankey's music sounds a little amateurish when we run across it in today's hymnals. But that is not his fault; he was pragmatic enough to sing and write what the people of his time would respond to.

His first attempt at writing a tune was a traumatic experience. While in Scotland in 1874, he spotted a poem, "The Ninety and Nine," in a newspaper. It was the story of John 10, the rescue of one lost sheep.

"I carefully read it over," Sankey wrote later, "and at once made up my mind that this would make a great hymn for evangelistic work — if it had a tune. . . . I cut out the poem and placed it in my scrapbook."

Two days later, Moody preached at a noon meeting on "The Good Shepherd," then called on Sankey, who was sitting at the harmonium, for a closing hymn. His mind was blank. He thought of the Twenty-third Psalm, but that had already been sung twice in the meeting. Something inside him said, "Sing the hymn you found on the train!"

He pulled out the clipping, struck an A-flat chord and fearfully began to sing, making up a tune as he went. He got through the first verse, and was afraid the next one would sound entirely different — but it didn't. The crowd was spellbound.

After the last, dramatic verse ("Rejoice, for the Lord brings back his own!") it seemed that "a great sigh seemed to go up from the meeting," Sankey said later. Moody, in tears, rushed to pick up the slip of newsprint and said, "Sankey, where did you get that hymn? I never heard the like of it in my life!"

Later that year, he wrote the music for "For You I Am Praying," followed eventually by "Faith Is the Victory," "When the Mists Have Rolled Away" and "A Shelter in the Time of Storm." But "The Ninety and Nine" remained his special solo; it seldom failed to hush even hostile audiences. Moody said that fifty percent of the credit for his success should go to Sankey — and that made it easier to face critics such as one prominent Irish minister who told him, "Stop using those catchy tunes before you have all the people dancing."

The same kinds of tales could be told of Homer Rodeheaver, Wendell P. Loveless and John W. Peterson in the present century as they edged toward the sounds of the swing era and its big bands. Their new "special music" was scorned as "night-clubbish." Why all the flak? From the third century to the twentieth, the pattern is the same: church music gradually abandoning the ordinary man, leaving him without a ready medium for worship, and then some brave soul trying to fill the vacuum and get back in touch by writing music laymen can quickly grasp — and getting kicked in the teeth for it.

Perhaps the answer lies in understanding the two tracks of music. Ever since the Renaissance, and possibly even before, there has been *serious* or *classical* music and *popular* or *"hit"* music.

The church has always been very big in the classical track, thanks to men like Pope Gregory, Palestrina, Bach, Purcell, Beethoven, Schubert, Brahms, and other professional composers. Classical music is technical; you have to know some details to know what's going on. It is also *timeless* (or at least the composer hopes it will be!), made for all generations and centuries to appreciate.

No problem there. But some Christians have also at times gotten into the popular track, the simple music of the masses. Here, techniques aren't nearly so crucial; most of the listeners know only that "it sounds good; I like it" — and that's enough.

Popular music, of course, is very *timely;* its styles are constantly changing. It's throw-away music. No one song lasts very long; it's big for a brief period, then fades quickly into oblivion as something else develops. In rock, the cycle takes less than six months; in other genres, a couple of years.

Thus, what St. Ambrose created to appeal to the masses was very different from what Luther created for the same purpose. Watts' and Wesley's "popular" hymns don't sound at all like Sankey's. But in their day, each was "right on."

Here comes the sticky part. Inevitably, the people who respond to a certain kind of church music on the popular track don't realize that it's popular and therefore temporary, *and don't want to give it up!* They want to hold on to it, keep it alive, preserve it as if it were timeless classical music. Charles Wesley may have scribbled off something riding along on his horse, but to Methodists for a hundred years after his death, it was almost Holy Writ. In America today, many Protestants are still clinging to the last great catch-up brought about by Sankey and his contemporaries. If Sankey were alive today, he would probably say, "Forget my stuff! It's not that great. Write some of your own that's current with what's happening in the popular track in your time."

The popular track keeps moving, always changing, always innovating for better or worse. Fortunately, since 1965 we have seen another great catch-up in our music as people like Ralph Carmichael, Otis Skillings, Kurt Kaiser, Ronn Huff, Jimmy Owens and Tedd Smith have done exactly like Luther and Watts and begun writing music in the current idiom. (They've also drawn about as many sparks.)

Whether we will repeat the error of our forefathers and cherish their "hits" as though they were classics — until they are hopelessly out of date — remains to be seen.

CHAPTER SIX

There's a new noise in the church these days,
young voices—and not just
junior choirs echoing their elders, either.

Sounds like those
from Rosemary
Nachtigall (left),
who cut her first
solo album at
age eighteen, and
a Youth for Christ
Teen Team (above)
which made two
tours to Europe
within a year, has
kids listening
for a change.

Junior high kids
with hands hardly large enough to reach
around a guitar neck . . .
all the way up to college students at an
Inter-Varsity conference at Urbana (right) . . .
have turned on to
the latest catch-up in music about God.

Isn't that some kind of beautiful?

THE LATEST CATCH-UP

For more decades than anyone would like to admit, a heavy nylon rope has been hog-tied around the bag of tricks every time it came to church. In some churches the knot was tied tighter than in others, but all had their restrictions.

In Catholic churches, only the organ sounds got out of the bag. Everything else was taboo; it wasn't "worthy" of God. The same went for some of the more formal Protestants.

A large number of Protestants allowed organ and piano. Some others were daring enough to let violins or flutes or trumpets out into the open, provided they behaved themselves. Even so, everyone sat nervously until they finished.

Then there were always those lower-class groups (poor, uncultured hillbillies!) with no sense of taste who let ungodly things like guitars and trombones and accordions out of the bag of sounds while in church. Sensing the frowns of the middle- and upper-class congregations across town, they, of course, tried to keep their instruments from swinging too much, like "the world."

Well, the church music revolution which has been going on since around 1965 is — thank the Lord and everyone else who had anything to do with it — *a liberation of the bag of tricks.* Christians have discovered (or rediscovered) that there is nothing intrinsically evil about a drum, or a string bass, or an amplified guitar, or a tambourine . . . or even a kazoo, for that matter! The composers have been turned loose to use almost any sound they wish, and not too many people are sleeping through it.

We have to stop right here and say that it's not only impossible but stupid to try to write an instant history of the current catch-up. With the avalanche of new records and music books, no one can immediately listen to everything that's being done. Every reader of this book has his favorites, of course. Someday in 1997, a university professor can write an exhaustive recount of what really happened back there in the late '60s and '70s, and the truth will be known. Until then, most accounts will be lop-sided in one way or another.

Some of the raw elements the professor will consider, however, will probably be these:

1. *Catholics, Episcopalians and other formalists have turned on to folk music.* As early as 1956, an East London vicar told composer Geoffrey Beaumont that he was "deeply concerned that nothing had been written since the Elizabethans, which can properly be called a folk mass." He said the music of the Anglican church was totally foreign to the majority of Englishmen, and so Beaumont responded by writing *Folk Mass* in a pop style.

But what really threw the doors open was the very first pronouncement of Vatican II. On December 4, 1963, by a vote of 2,147 churchmen to 4, the Roman Catholic hierarchy said it wouldn't be such a bad idea to use English (or the native language) instead of Latin for certain parts of the Mass. It also recommended singing by the people.

That was all it took. The very day the English translation of the Mass was released, Ray Repp, a student at Kenrick Seminary in St. Louis, sat down and put the whole thing to folk guitar music. He played it for his seminary buddies as a joke — but they liked it, and began to circulate it underground. Two years later, it was recorded by F.E.L. Publications, Ltd. (Friends of the English Liturgy), which has continued to be a major outlet of guitar masses and other liturgical folk pieces. F.E.L.'s "Hymnal for Young Christians" has sold over four million copies.

Father Peter Scholtes did a mass in bossa nova style, and again people liked it. He also wrote a quiet thing called, "They'll Know We Are Christians by Our Love" which, after a few years, spread far beyond the Catholic church.

The Dameans . . . Sister Miriam Therese Winter and the Medical Mission Sisters of Philadelphia . . . The Roamin' Brothers (get the pun?) . . . and many others are putting soft, folk sounds to the Church's liturgy. The lyrics remain untouched, exactly as dictated by the hierarchy, but the sounds have been nothing short of revolutionary to people who've grown up with the Gregorian chant.

A group of students evidences the great leap forward in Catholic music.

A Chicago group called "The Exceptions" has even done a "Rock 'n' Roll Mass" with a fairly heavy sound. They couldn't resist a few additions here and there ("Christ, have mercy — yeah, yeah, yeah.") Well-known artists Duke Ellington and Dave Brubeck have tried their hands at writing religious music in jazz styles, and Leonard Bernstein's *Mass* was a rather bizarre opener in 1971 for the new John F. Kennedy Center for the Performing Arts in Washington, D.C.

2. *The more informal Protestants have opened up gradually as well.* If you want to choose a starting point, you might select Billy Graham's 1965 film, *The Restless Ones.* It was one of the first Christian movies intentionally made for theaters instead of churches, and the music by Ralph Carmichael included a rollicking song called "He's Everything to Me." Carmichael had been in religious music in the early '50s with some big band sounds and ran into enough flak from traditionalists that he dropped out of sight for a few years to work in secular music. But with *The Restless Ones,* he came back, and this time the evangelical world (at least the under-30s) were ready to listen to him. The next year, Graham did another

film, *For Pete's Sake*, which included an intense solo, "The Man," probably Carmichael's best set of lyrics so far.

The first folk musicals came along in 1968: *Good News*, popular among Southern Baptists, and *Tell It Like It Is*, a collaboration between Carmichael and Kurt Kaiser. They weren't real brainy, but at least the sound was refreshing, and *Tell It* wound up with a moving suggestion, "Pass It On." It sold over 300,000 copies in the first three years, as hundreds of local youth choirs staged it. The next year, the same two men did *Natural High*, Otis Skillings came through with *Life*, then *Love*, and Jimmy and Carol Owens did *Show Me*. Tedd Smith, Graham's pianist, jumped out of his traditional gospel track with *New Vibrations and Requiem for a Nobody*.

The demand was great enough for groups to travel the country full-time: The Spurrlows . . . Campus Crusade's New Folk . . . the Continentals, who deliberately shocked some people by doing an entire album of

Duke Ellington's jazz band sends new vibrations through the Cathedral of St. John the Divine in New York City during a special performance of Ellington's "Sacred Concert."

Soul Concern, one of nearly fifty Youth for Christ teams to travel in the United States and overseas since 1961, hams it up under a bridge.

old hymns in rock idiom (shades of the past!). Oral Roberts' World Action Singers first appeared on national television in March 1969. Youth for Christ International started in the same year with the New World Singers, the Young and Free, then Steve and Maria, Random Sample, Trust Company and Soul Concern.

Southern gospel quartets have, of course, traveled professionally ever since the '30s — but Southern gospel music is a different world from that of the Carmichael fan. Northerners tend to look down their noses at the quartet style ("inferior . . . shall not be permitted" is the way the Baptist Bible College of Pennsylvania feels about it).

But the religious music tycoons know there's big money in Southern gospel, and so does RCA, which has recorded the quartets for years. What keeps the field so fertile is that, unlike most other religious styles, it is based on a "hit" psychology. Nobody tries to preserve the oldies. New songs are constantly being written and performed, which keep the fans buying records, which keep the groups' big buses on the road.

Southern gospel didn't have a revolution in the late '60s like everything else — it didn't need it. It has always stayed current with the sounds and patterns of its secular counterpart, country and western music. The only changes have been the addition of drums to some groups (wisely called "gospel drums" for the benefit of the little old ladies). If you dig country and western, you dig Southern gospel. The words get pretty hackneyed at times in both fields. But both are constantly evolving. It's as simple as that.

One quartet, the Oak Ridge Boys, was among the first religious groups to capitalize on the folk trend with a 1965 album called "Folk Minded Spirituals for Spiritual Minded Folk." The Imperials, started by ex-Statesmen Quartet lead singer Jake Hess, has branched almost away from Southern gospel into a smooth Lettermen-type sound all their own.

3. *Some very good soloists have appeared.* When rock cooled down around 1969 and the big groups began to break up, it was once again permissible to sing by yourself with just a guitar. Some people like Ray Hildebrand, Dallas Holm, Linda Rich, Gene Cotton and John Fischer are doing just that and very well. Instead of being big-production, they're just themselves . . . and what they simply try to say comes off strong at times.

Of course, Cliff Richard, the British rock 'n' roll star who shocked the world by claiming Christ during a Billy Graham crusade in June 1966, is in a class by himself. He was the English version of Elvis Presley, on top of the charts around the world everywhere except in the United States since 1958. Despite all his talking and singing about his faith, he was still named 1971's Outstanding Singer by the Songwriters' Guild of Great Britain.

4. *A great second surge has come along with the music of the Jesus Movement.* The main differences in Jesus music are in the lyrics (it's street language) and in the fact that nobody here is afraid of a straight rock sound. Not all of it is solid rock, of course, but some is. The whole scene is considerably more natural and unpretentious than what came earlier, probably because Jesus groups don't think as much about church deacons looking over their shoulders.

Andrae Crouch and the Disciples . . . Larry Norman . . . Randy Matthews . . . The Armageddon Experience . . . Love Song . . . Agape . . . Sound Foundation . . . Danny Lee and the Children of Truth are just a few of the names. In massive festivals all over the country, young people are introduced to Jesus Christ through their straightforward music.

What it all adds up to is that for the first time since Sankey, we've got a big batch of music that non-Christians can identify with. The Scott Ross Show, for example, is a two-hour syndicated radio program in the rock format currently being heard on over seventy rock stations. Ross, a former deejay and emcee at one of the Beatles' historic Shea Stadium concerts, is a shoot-from-the-hip guy lays on the Gospel in between songs. A sample half hour in late 1971:

"Family Affair"	Sly and the Family Stone
"Wind-Up"	Jethro Tull
"Don't Go Near the Water"	Beach Boys
"Love"	Lettermen
"Let Your Light Shine On"	Michael Rabon & Choctaw
"Light in the Night"	Red, Wilder, Blue
"Morning Has Broken"	Cat Stevens
"Jesus Is the Key"	Ken Christy & the Sunday People
"If You Will Believe"	The Way

The encouraging point is that Ross can even find enough *questioning* music from the secular rock scene and *answering* music from the Jesus scene to fill two hours every week. The rock stations are generally happy to fulfill their religious programming (required by the FCC) with such a show.

5. *Frankly, the lyrics so far haven't been as good as the sounds.* There's still a lot of amateurish, empty phrases. Some of the cliches persist. Now that the ropes are completely off the bag of tricks, a few people are starting to pay more attention to writing heavier words to replace the earlier pablum.

For example, Larry Norman's "I Wish We'd All Been Ready" said a lot in a new way:

Life was filled with guns and war,
And everyone got trampled on the floor.
I wish we'd all been ready.
Children died, the days grew cold,
A piece of bread could buy a bag of gold,
I wish we'd all been ready.

There's no time to change your mind,
The Son has come, and you've been left behind. . . .

"Dressing Up Jesus," from an album named *Our Front Porch* produced by *Campus Life* Magazine with Ralph Carmichael, hit the modern rationalizations about Jesus:

Everybody's dressin' up Jesus,
Style Him just like you want Him to be.
Everybody's dressin' up Jesus now,
You're just seein' what you're wantin' to see.
Let Him keep His sandals,
Robe and flowing hair;
Now you add some red and yellow beads.
Cover up the callouses,
Keep Him thin and fair,
A little speech on love and peace is really all He needs.

Cliff Richard, the English superstar, during a Yugoslav press conference.

(Chorus)
> *Where is Jesus? Who's side is He on?*
> *Where is Jesus? Wonder where He's gone.*
> *Would you know Him if He stood up now?*
> *Finding Jesus — can you tell me how, tell me how?*
> *Have you really seen Him? Looked at Him straight on?*
> *Can you take Him as He is with the trimmings and trappings gone?*

The counterculture isn't alone, though, in holding distortions about Christ. The next two verses:

> *Everybody's dressin' up Jesus,*
> *He looks fine in "Establishment Gray."*
> *Everybody's cuttin' up Jesus now,*
> *See His hair — you'll have to trim it away.*
> *Up in high society, He knows what to do;*
> *After all He really is a king.*
> *Quote His words of wisdom, join the chosen few,*
> *And keep your Jesus dignified, the image is the thing.*

(Chorus)

A man and his mike:
Scott Ross.

Everybody's dressin' up Jesus,
Get your brush, are you ready to paint?
Everybody's touchin' up Jesus now,
Make Him Afro or a dashiki saint.
Brighten up His seamless robe, darken up His skin;
Keep His eyes of black and keep His soul.
Red and yellow, black and white, which one's gonna win?
I guess you'll have to wait and find out when they call the roll.
(Chorus)[1]

To describe the good vibrations of the Jesus Movement, Love Song, a California band, wrote "Little Country Church":

They're talkin' 'bout revival and the need for love,
That little church has come alive.

114

Workin' with each other for the common good,
Puttin' all the past aside.
Long hair, short hair, some coats and ties,
People finally comin' around,
Lookin' past the hair and straight into the eyes,
People finally comin' around.

And it's very plain to see
It's not the way it used to be. [2]

How much of this latest catch-up will last? Very little, say some critics, who claim that much of it is mediocre and will soon fade.

So what else is new? They fail to remember that most of Luther's and Watts' catch-ups were mediocre, too. Only the most outstanding hymns survived.

Actually, it might not be the worst thing for the Carmichael sound and Jesus-rock to fade — because they're popular, not classical. If Christians in the year 2000 are still singing "One in the Spirit," they may be far out of it. In fact, it's probably already time to throw away "He's Everything to Me" as well as others from 1965-68. They were great songs during that period — but now, maybe they should rest in peace, and be replaced with what's *now*.

The popular track of music continues its irresistible march, and so should music about God.

The gates and fences have been kicked aside . . .
God's world is wide open.
Run! Sing! Cavort! Explore! Express!
That's what God did when He made this planet.
He had an absolute extravaganza all by Himself
creating surf and jonquils and koala bears and . . .
then man "in His own image."
Man . . . the one being to create,
producing ideas and art and music out of nothing.
Let creativity roll on!

LET'S FOOL 'EM THIS TIME

Is there any good reason why music about God (of the popular variety) needs to fall behind once again? Must Christians canonize the current catch-up and engrave it in holy stone? Is there anything keeping us from putting Jesus' message in the formats people will understand best in 1980? 1985?

Nothing. Nothing except our history.

If, however, we are to actually break the historical cycle and stay flexible and current this time around, we are going to have to understand a few things about creativity. After all, here's what we're up against, as outlined by the English writer Dorothy Sayers:

"The Church as a body has never made up her mind about the arts, and it is hardly too much to say that she has never tried. She has, of course, from time to time puritanically denounced the arts as irreligious and mischievous, or tried to exploit the arts as a means to the teaching of religion and morals — but . . . both these attitudes are false and degrading."

We'll get a lot farther if we can dig the following:

1. *There's really nothing wrong with expressing artistically what God is doing.* God is essentially a Spirit, but He doesn't mind at all being portrayed in visual or audible ways. In fact, His world of nature shows Him to be the most ambitious artist of all.

A mere twenty years ago some Protestants were still denouncing all fiction because it was not "real." A hundred years ago girls at Mt. Holyoke College in Massachusetts were not allowed "to devote more than one hour a week to miscellaneous reading. The *Atlantic Monthly,* Shakespeare, Scott's novels, Robinson Crusoe and immoral works are strictly forbidden," said the rules of conduct.

2. *But if we misuse the arts as propaganda tools, we spoil them.* Music and painting, poetry and drama weren't really made for clubbing people over the head with a "message." They are avenues of self-expression — and if what you express through your music (your exhilaration because of Jesus, for example) is a great new idea to someone else, that's a welcome by-product. But if, on the other hand, the only reason you sing is to impress the other person, the whole interchange falls a little flat and phony.

Creative art is a flashlight in this dark world, not a cattle prod.

3. *Truth sometimes pops up in odd places.* During World War II, the Nazis had a slight problem of what to do about the obviously superb classical music written by Jews — Mendelssohn, for example. It was downright painful for them to have to recognize excellence from that kind of source! So they had the music printed with only the word "Anonymous" at the top of the page, or else they banned it altogether.

Well, a man doesn't have to be a Nazi to write quality music or do other outstanding things. Nor does he have to be a Christian. A surgeon may be a wife-beater or a drunk — and still be able to save your life. A professor may have twisted ideas about God, but know a great deal about calculus. A rock group may be fairly crude and indecent, and yet quite articulate in describing alienation or loneliness.

The Christian doesn't need to let this bother him. People are simply smart in some areas and stupid in others, that's all. We can benefit from brilliance wherever we find it, while ignoring spots where the same people don't know what they're talking about.

Thomas á Kempis, the fifteenth century monk, once wrote that if a man's heart is right and his mind attuned to God's perspective, then everything he sees and hears becomes "a book of holy teaching." Granted, the monastery he lived in didn't have newsstands, movie marquees and radio stations quite like our world today! But his point is still valid; even the evil in life shows us what God is *unlike.* We can see trash as trash. Truth — even despairing, ugly truth — is put into perspective through Christ. We are to be virile plants on an alien planet, receiving our food and energy from the Son.

4. *If God's music is to stay caught up this time, young people are going to have to lead the way.* Not because they're more intelligent than older people, but because the times simply demand it. "The popular music

scene today is unlike any scene I can think of in the history of all music," says Leonard Bernstein. "It's completely of, by and for the kids, and by kids I mean anyone from eight years old to twenty-five. They write the songs, they sing them, own them, record them. They also buy the records, create the market, and they set the fashion in the music, in dress, in dance, in hair style, lingo, social attitudes."

Why not in church?

We cannot allow ourselves to be intimidated by the fact that most of the songs people sing today are already pressed in plastic or recorded on mylar or printed on glossy paper. We have to make a start anyway. The truth is that the big music moguls are hungry for new material, especially songs written by young people. In coffeehouses, in small ensembles, in campus clubs, kids are expressing themselves in music as naturally as most people express themselves doodling. And some of it eventually gets published. Even if it doesn't, the person who created it gets a great thrill out of turning a piece of himself into art, and sharing it with his listeners.

During the Reformation, more than a half-million hymns were written. A sudden spurt of song-writing has accompanied virtually every revival and renewal in church history. In contrast, the twentieth century has produced few hymns — just try to find more than a dozen or two in your average church hymnal by checking the dates. Now we've cranked up again, with folk songs and rock musicals replacing the hymn format. In order to keep it going, we're going to have to —

**Keep aware of what's happening musically, and synthesize.* There's no better way to do good work than to study other people's good work. That's the way any artist develops his creative talent.

That doesn't mean you copy! The Christian, particularly, does not blindly imitate the non-Christian world. Instead, he studies it, recognizes truth and genius wherever he finds it and uses what he sees to develop something even better.

**Go for variety.* The God who made geraniums, Airedales, quasars and fog is obviously a God of incredible diversity. His creativity, as poured through His people, is an unpredictable thing to behold. We see the drama and richness of life all around us, and that is the stuff of music.

We don't have to try to write "Christian music." *We write music —period* — as a Christian, and God's perspective can't help but show through, whether the topic is the fear of a boy whose parents are separating, the ecstasy of finding a lover thought to be dead, or the glimmer of a ghetto child finding that she really can succeed at something.

After all, the Bible is a wildly diverse book, not only in content, but also in style. God didn't give us 100 percent sermons from St. Paul; He mixed it up with poetry, first-person adventures, biography, all kinds of literature. It's rich; it doesn't fit into one narrow groove.

**Probe the enigmas, the mysteries.* Again, the Bible is not a book of pat answers. It leaves us scratching our heads often. It leaves loose ends and unfinished questions at times — that's why it's so intriguing. It shows life as it really is.

If we're honest in our music, we'll have to do the same. We simply don't have all the solutions to the world's problems. We know that Jesus does, but we don't always know His thinking from start to finish. Our brains couldn't grasp its complexity if He told us. Honesty about our blind spots and the difficulties we haven't yet figured out is a lot better than bluffing.

The orthodox Scripture followers of Jesus' day had all sorts of neat, tidy ideas about the Messiah. Many had it all mapped out just what He would do. He'd rise 300 feet over Jerusalem, then set up His city precisely on the measurements of Ezekiel's rod.

These men were reading the right prophecies. But when the Messiah came, He was so different, so unpredictable, that even Satan himself was faked out. Imagine — the Messiah died! He was executed! And then He rose from the dead!

You just can't put Jesus in a box.

**Work together.* Music about God is not supposed to be an ego trip. If one person can write poetry, and another can make up tunes, they should get together, expressing the unity of the body of Christ through music. The person who says he's not creative — he could never do anything musical — may be not only ignoring the virile freedom that characterized music in Bible times, but missing a chance to make something beautiful with a little help from his friends.

Perhaps it is significant that the Bible's songbook, the Psalms, ends with a wild, exultant paean of praise where everybody gets in on the act:

Praise ye the Lord!
Praise God in His sanctuary;
  Praise Him in His mighty firmament!
Praise Him for His mighty deeds;
  Praise Him according to His excelling greatness!
Praise Him with the trumpet blast;
  Praise Him with lyre and harp!
Praise Him with timbrel and processional;
  Praise Him on stringed instruments and flutes!
Praise Him with clashing cymbals;
  Praise Him with loud, clanging cymbals!
Let everything that has breath praise the Lord!
  Praise ye the Lord![1]

[1] Psalm 150. The Modern Language Bible The (New Berkeley Version) © 1969 by Zondervan Publishing House. Used by permission.

SOURCES

Records, news releases, promotion kits, statistics and photos from general trade companies (AM, Capitol, Columbia, Decca, United Artists, Warner Bros.) as well as religious producers (Avant-Garde, Creative Sound, F. E. L., FourMost, Impact/Benson, Inter-Varsity, Light/Word, Lorenz, Now Sounds/Singspiration, Radio and Television Commission/Southern Baptist Convention, Supreme, Tim Spencer, Vanguard).

Tapes from the Scott Ross Show as well as taped lectures by Bob Larson and Don Wyrtzen.

A mountain of clippings — features, interviews, news coverages — from *Time, Life, Hit Parader, Planet, New York, Saturday Review, Saturday Evening Post, Charlie,* the *Boston Globe,* the *Chicago Daily News,* the *Chicago Tribune Magazine.* Also comments and articles from Christian periodicals *(Baptist Bulletin, Campus Life, Catholic Home, Christian Life, Christianity Today, Decision, Eternity, Good News, Hollywood Free Paper, Renaissance, The Other Side, The Student, Today).*

Books, including:
Carl Belz, *The Story of Rock* (New York: Oxford University Press, 1969).

Armin Haeussler, *The Story of Our Hymns* (St. Louis: Eden Publishing Co., 1952).

Phil Kerr, *Music in Evangelism* (Glendale, Calif.: Gospel Music Publishers, 1939).

Dave Laing, *The Sound of Our Time* (Chicago: Quadrangle Books, 1969).

Bob Larson, *Hindus, Hippies and Rock and Roll* (self-published, 1969).

Bob Larson, *Rock and the Church* (Carol Stream, Ill.: Creation House, 1971).

Ira Peck, *The New Sound/Yes!* (New York: Four Winds, 1966).

John Pollock, *Moody* (Grand Rapids, Mich.: Zondervan Publishing Co., 1963).

Julius Portnoy, *Music in the Life of Man* (New York: Holt, Rinehart and Winston, 1963).

Lillian Roxon, *Rock Encyclopedia* (New York: Grosset and Dunlap, 1969).

John Rublowsky, *Popular Music* (New York: Basic Books, 1967).

Louis Savary, *Popular Song and Youth Today* (New York: Association Press, 1971).

Dorothy Sayers, *Christian Letters to a Post-Christian World* (Grand Rapids, Mich.: Eerdmans Publishing Co., 1969).

Alfred Sendrey and Mildred Norton, *David's Harp* (New York: NAL-World, 1964).

David Winter, *New Singer, New Song* (Waco, Texas: Word Books, 1967).

Naturally, every volume (or almost) of *Encyclopedia Britannica* as well as *Who Was Who in America*, the *National Cyclopedia, American Peoples Encyclopedia* and half a dozen research reports from Britannica's Library Research Service.